# HEAVEN'S MORNING

**The Bible Reading Fellowship**
15 The Chambers, Vineyard
Abingdon OX14 3FE
brf.org.uk

BRF is a Registered Charity (233280)

ISBN 978 0 85746 476 7
First published 2016
Reprinted 2016
10 9 8 7 6 5 4 3 2 1
All rights reserved

Cover image: © iStock

**Acknowledgements**
Unless otherwise stated, scripture quotations are taken from The New Revised Standard Version of
the Bible, Anglicised Edition, copyright © 1989, 1995 by the Division of Christian Education of the
National Council of the Churches of Christ in the USA, are used by permission. All rights reserved.

Extracts from the Authorised Version of the Bible (The King James Bible), the rights in which are
vested in the Crown, are reproduced by permission of the Crown's Patentee, Cambridge University
Press.

Extracts from the New Jerusalem Bible © 1985 by Darton, Longman & Todd Ltd and Doubleday,
a division of Bantam Doubleday Dell Publishing Group, Inc.

Every effort has been made to trace and contact copyright owners for material used in this
resource. We apologise for any inadvertent omissions or errors, and would ask those concerned to
contact us so that full acknowledgement can be made in the future.

A catalogue record for this book is available from the British Library

Printed and bound by CPI Group (UK) Ltd, Croydon CR0 4YY

# HEAVEN'S MORNING

## Rethinking the destination

## David Winter

# Contents

# Final flight

*No suitcase? Surely a small holdall*
*with my best jacket, smart shoes?*
*No footwear? What of my family photo*
*in the silver frame? My certificates?*
*How do I prove my worth? Passport,*
*bank statement, title deeds?*

*No sharp objects, nothing flammable,*
*no textiles, nothing practical,*
*no paper, card or plastic, no money,*
*no jewels, not even a wedding ring,*
*no liquids or solids,*
*no laptop, phone or sweets;*
*just follow the light.*

*Leave memories behind*
*but take humility, take firm belief.*
*With empty hands to nurture prayer,*
*seek the pearly glow at take-off.*

*Zero baggage allowed.*

C. SHEILA GRUNDY
FINALIST IN JACK CLEMO POETRY AWARDS 2011

# Introduction

> *Modern man, if he dared to be articulate about his concept of heaven, would describe a vision which would look like the biggest department store in the world, showing new things and gadgets, and himself having plenty of money with which to buy them.*
>
> Erich Fromm, *The Sane Society* (1955)

The undertakers phoned. An elderly man in my parish had died and the widow wanted a church funeral. I knew the house but was pretty sure that I had never seen any of its occupants in church. I rang the bell and a woman who had obviously been crying opened the door. We went into a cosy parlour and I asked about her husband. She was keen to talk—how she'd constantly urged him to go to the doctor, but he was so stubborn ('There's nothing wrong with me but a bit of indigestion'). Finally, he agreed to go to the GP but by then it was too late. He was in hospital a week and died there.

She was still numb from the shock of it all, but eventually I had to raise the question of the funeral. Had she any particular wishes about it—people to speak, perhaps, or special music that her husband loved? She thought for a moment. 'Well, vicar, we don't want anything miserable.'

Some gentle questioning established what she meant by 'miserable'. She didn't want anything that would upset family and friends. Basically, when you reduced it to essentials, she didn't want us to talk about death.

She'd made a few notes on a sheet of paper to explain what she had in mind. Someone from his golf club to tell a few funny stories about his experiences on the links. A couple of his favourite songs—'I Did It My Way', for one. Perhaps one of the grandchildren reading a poem about grandpas. 'But no "dust to dust". Please,' she said firmly. I pointed out that I was bound to use the regular funeral service, which she accepted, but was anxious that people who came already 'upset' should not be made to feel worse.

Eventually we agreed on the service, but in fact we both compromised. She agreed to several prayers that spoke fairly clearly about the reality of death and the sense of loss it inevitably entails. I agreed to do the graveside committal in the town cemetery with the aid of the undertakers while everybody else went off for refreshments in the local pub. I don't think either of us was entirely happy with these arrangements, but in the event the service was for me recognisably Christian and for her the reading (Revelation 21:1–5, with the words 'he will wipe every tear from their eyes') evoked a positive response. 'It's like a lovely poem,' she said, and I agreed.

That was over 20 years ago, in the days when virtually all funerals were conducted by ministers of religion. Since then that scenario, familiar to clergy and undertakers and accepted by relatives who expected at least the formality of a religious ceremony, has slowly given way to a new one, in which church and religion are carefully excluded. The advent of secular 'celebrants' has given families (and undertakers) a way to sidestep any notion of a religious rite and to replace it with a kind of public tribute with songs. This does at least accurately mirror the spirit of the age, which finds the whole business of death a painful reminder that no matter how clever we may be technologically and medically, this is how it inevitably ends.

This book is an attempt to address the issues raised by that situation. Do Christians simply accept the situation, recognising that belief in things like resurrection, eternal life and heaven is now a minority interest of 'religious' people? Or can we re-present the issue of death and the 'hereafter' in terms that can make sense to people in a world not only vastly different from that of biblical times, but from that of a mere 20, 30 or 40 years ago? As followers of a faith whose basic tenet is that its Founder rose from the dead, and promised 'eternal life' to those who believed in him, it is, as they say, a 'no-brainer'.

## Facing the final curtain

The modern world, and even the Church in that setting, struggles to make sense of the whole business of death, dying, judgement and the 'hereafter'. People have spotted that hardly anybody actually believes the traditional stuff about heaven and hell any more. On the other hand, some deep residual instinct makes it hard for them to sign up to a complete rejection of the idea of a life beyond this one. So, even at a 'secular' funeral service, people cheerfully talk of their loved ones who have 'passed on' (in the tentative language favoured by relatives) as somehow being 'Up There', fully conversant with the football results and the arrival of a new grandchild. Vera Lynn ends the service with 'We'll meet again, don't know where, don't know when', but for many people it's just wishful thinking—a gentle subterfuge to avoid a harsh reality.

If Christians wish to convince a scientific, sceptical and largely secular generation that to believe in heaven is anything more than that, they can't hide any longer behind ideas and images that are the products of a long-past tradition rather than the actual teaching of Jesus and the apostles. We believe in resurrection, not resuscitation. We look for a *new* heaven and a *new* earth, not the old one extended. Our hope is the kingdom of God, not more of what we've got already. We believe in eternal life, not everlasting existence.

When people speak of their loved ones as 'Up There' it bears little relation to the traditional Christian teaching about heaven (let alone hell). It's simply a second innings on a better pitch with nothing fundamentally changed. By and large, and sadly, Christian ministers (and I include myself) have felt bound to buy into this pathetic dilution of the glorious vision of the kingdom of heaven.

There is a general reluctance in our Western society to think seriously about the possibility that there really is a life beyond this one, a transformation (not an extension) of our present life in an utterly new environment. The challenge of comprehending or putting into a belief system an entirely 'other' way of self-conscious being, which is what the Bible offers, stretches our credulity to breaking point. We find ourselves stuck between the ineffable and the incredible.

Yet it is still an important question. The issue of life beyond this life—'eternal life', in biblical language—is crucial to our understanding of who we are and what purpose we inhabit in the creation. It offers one answer, at least, to Stephen Hawking's haunting question, 'Why does the universe bother to exist?'

# A voice from another world?

Fifty years ago I wrote a short book called *Hereafter*, in which I sought to present the traditional Christian doctrines of eternal life for as wide an audience as possible. It turned out to be the only genuine 'bestseller' of my literary career (about a quarter of a million copies worldwide). When this present book was mooted I got that one down off the shelf and read it again. It sounded like a voice from another world. It's not that what it set out was demonstrably untrue or false, but that it was strangely irrelevant. The answers may not have changed, but the questions have. The present book is my attempt, in the radically different environment of the early 21st century, to re-examine for the present generation our understanding of the great Christian vision of God's ultimate purpose for humankind, and to do it in a way that respects both the magnificent revelation which the Bible offers and the honesty and openness of the questions modern people ask.

# Chapter One

## Visions and metaphors

> *All we know of what they do above,*
> *Is that they happy are, and that they*
> *love.*
>
> Edmund Waller, 'Upon the Death of my
> Lady Rich' (1645)

I remember, probably 60 years ago, visiting a woman in a tiny flat in Tottenham, north London. The area was run-down, the flats had been condemned and were awaiting demolition, the staircase was dirty and her room was small. She was, however, despite various disabilities, a shining example of simple Christian faith. She apologised for her dingy surroundings, but in fact her smile lit up the whole scene. As we were leaving (having at her request prayed with her), she said cheerily, 'Never mind. I'll have a mansion in heaven.' She was, of course, referring to the words of Jesus in the old King James Version of the Bible: 'In my Father's house are many mansions… I go to prepare a place for you' (John 14:2). Although even then I knew it was a misleading translation, I cherished for a long while the thought of her being escorted to number 51 Pearly Gates Way.

Churchgoers in those days were still familiar with the language of Victorian hymns, with their reunions 'at the river', the 'knitting severed friendships up', the 'home for little children above the bright blue sky'. 'The countless host' still streamed through 'the gates of pearl'. The language was unambiguous and the hope confident, at any rate in song and liturgy. Clergy committed the body of the deceased to the grave (as we still do) 'in sure and certain hope of the resurrection to eternal life'.

Yet slowly the old certainties were put to severe tests. It's hard to put a date on it, but somewhere in the generation that grew up after World War II a note of doubt began to sound. It can probably best be represented by the sort of questions Christian ministers and preachers found themselves being asked. 'Why do we talk of heaven as "above" or in the skies? We have probed the solar system and far beyond and know now that space is vast, possibly infinite—but there are no signs of a heavenly city.' 'Why do we say in the Creed that we believe in "the resurrection of the body"? Which body? Surely not this one?' 'How could heaven possibly be vast enough to accommodate all its potential inhabitants? Does "heaven" just go on for ever and ever, millennia after millennia?'

Behind these rather obvious questions lies another, more serious one. It was put to me in a funeral visit by a woman who greeted me by saying that she wasn't a Christian, but her husband, who had just died, was. Temporarily thrown by her frankness, I asked about his illness, the visits to hospital, and how their family had taken his death. Suddenly she interrupted this trivial avoidance of the big question. 'Vicar,' she said, 'do you believe in life after death?' I paused to frame a reply, but before I could she looked me in the face and said, 'No, honestly.'

In one sense questions of the general kind are simply unanswerable. No one knows, or could know. Her question, on the other hand, was stark in its simplicity. Did I, a Christian minister bound by my vows to preach and teach the faith, actually—really, without doubt or caveat—believe what it taught about eternal life? I can't remember what I said on that occasion, though I know I did assure her that I believed, as I still do, in the reality of the resurrection and the promise of the kingdom of heaven. I don't think she was convinced, though she was too polite to say so.

In fact the testimony of the Bible, the creeds and Christian tradition can't, with the best will in the world, be reduced to a series of propositions about a mode of existence—a way of 'being'—which is literally beyond our comprehension. But until modern people are offered a vision of eternal life which does not require them to treat visions like concrete facts, and metaphors like an instruction manual, the tide of scepticism (or honest doubt) will continue to rise. I left that woman's home a wiser, and possibly more sensitive, advocate of the Christian case.

Most people have picked up a distorted, or at any rate diminished, idea of the traditional Christian teaching on life beyond death: Peter at the Pearly Gates, guarding the entrance and using his 'keys' to let some in and exclude others; the hot fires of hell, where sinners are destined to perish; the longed-for reunions with those we have loved and lost. Some of the ideas are so unpleasant that they are automatically dismissed as incompatible with the notion of a God of compassion and mercy. Some are so wonderfully desirable that they are dismissed as wishful thinking. The result is that 'heaven' is reduced to a vague hope that somehow things will turn out for the best: 'All shall be well, and all manner of thing shall be well', as the great Mother Julian put it eight centuries ago.

Yet the idea of heaven persists, like an earwig in our collective memory. Even secular and humanist funerals find themselves slipping into its images and echoes. I recall a humanist memorial service at which one tribute referred to 'Neil and Mary up there arguing about today's editorial in *The Guardian*'. Of course, if challenged the speaker would have strongly rejected any idea of such an occurrence as a factual event, yet it does seem very hard for human beings to avoid the feeling that life is so powerful a condition that it can't simply be permanently terminated by the death of the body.

After all, every human culture that we know of has its own version of the 'hereafter', a place or mode of being where life is still celebrated and enjoyed. From the Valhalla of the Norsemen, the Elysian Fields of the Greeks and Romans, the Buddhist nirvana and the Egyptian 'abode of the dead' to the Jewish 'Abraham's Bosom' and the Christian 'kingdom of heaven' there is ample evidence of the stubborn durability of the notion that this life is not all there is.

*The Times* columnist Matthew Parris is the kind of thoughtful humanist who scratches where our preconceived ideas itch. In a brilliant article (*The Times*, 30 May 2015) he argued that what he called the feeling that 'we're part of a future we won't be in' is inbred in human beings, 'a primal fact, no more "true" or "false" than sexual attraction'. All the rest, he argued, 'all the rational intellectual stuff, all the reasoning, all the searching, all the books of metaphysics, the what's-it-all-about speculation over a life hereafter... all the tracts about pearly gates, the last judgment and heaven and hell... is a consequence, not a cause of our gut feeling that there's more to it than our short lives. There has to be something: we feel it in our very marrow.' His argument is intriguing: there has to be something, but there isn't. All that we have is an inbred instinct, a primal fact, which expresses itself in many different forms of religious and philosophical belief.

Among all the options in that supermarket of ideas and beliefs about what happens after death the Christian case has proved the most marketable for the last two millennia. However, it quickly developed from the teaching of Jesus and his apostles as we find it in the New Testament into a system of belief which is now widely questioned. From the 'kingdom of heaven' of Jesus, or the 'new creation' of which the apostles spoke, church history has formulated a complex and at times contradictory system of beliefs. These have been expressed in creed and liturgy and celebrated in hymns and great musical works like Fauré's *Requiem* or Handel's *Messiah*. When people today say that they 'can't believe' the Church's teaching on life after death, it is usually this formulation which they are rejecting.

Examples of the problem are not hard to find. How could anyone have ever thought in terms of 'years in purgatory', when time ceases the moment I die? What do we mean when we sing or pray about 'everlasting' life, when we will have moved out of this space-time universe into the world of eternity? Is it helpful to speak of our belief in 'the resurrection of the body' without at least recognising that the Bible offers no future at all for the physical body which one day will be buried or burnt? 'Flesh and blood cannot inherit the kingdom of God,' said Paul rather bluntly (1 Corinthians 15:50). Before we can move on to rebuild a credible doctrine of life after death we need to do a demolition job on ideas which try to lock eternity into the language of earth.

## Metaphors of the kingdom

When Jesus spoke of the 'kingdom of heaven' (as Matthew calls it), or the 'kingdom of God', in Mark and Luke, he invariably did so in metaphors and similes: 'the kingdom of heaven is *like…*' In doing so, he was using the preaching method of the Jewish rabbi, who expects his disciples to bring to the learning experience their own degree of faith, understanding and imagination. So these sayings were often ended with the strange injunction, 'Those who have ears to hear, let them hear.' The metaphor (or its expanded version, a 'parable') had been spoken. Now it was time for the faithful seeker after the truth to dwell on it until its implicit message had been received and understood.

I recall that great broadcaster Rabbi Lionel Blue once pointing up a difference between this rabbinical approach and that of many Christian preachers. In the pulpit many ministers will also tell a story (a 'parable'), but then they spoil it all by explaining it. That was not the way of Jesus. 'Here is the metaphor, here is the story: now reflect on it until you feel you have grasped its meaning.'

The kingdom metaphors in the Gospels come thick and

fast, especially in Matthew, and they form a fascinating complex of images and ideas about the 'kingdom of heaven'. It will be like new wine, like good seed, like yeast in a bowl of flour, like a pearl of great price, like unexpected treasure found buried in a field, like a huge net catching all kinds of fish, like a wedding banquet, like a mustard seed, and—perhaps most vividly of all, captured not only in words but in a living visual aid—the kingdom of God is an unsophisticated child, utterly dependent and utterly trusting.

The trouble for modern readers of the Bible is that we don't like having to work at metaphors. We expect the Gospels to be more practical and instructive than that: explanations that we can readily understand, instructions we can simply follow, promises we can eagerly claim. But that is precisely what they are not. This is ultimate truth in the form of a story—I would say, the greatest story ever told. This is the revelation of the purposes of our Creator, not set out as propositions, but as pictures.

This has two consequences. The 'story' the Gospels tell is both incredibly simple (so that a child, familiar with the world of the story, can understand) and incredibly profound, so that a lifetime's study does not exhaust its significance.

A writer in my position is tempted to go through all the metaphors Jesus used about the kingdom of heaven and try to 'explain' them. That, however, would be to distort the intentions of the rabbi-prophet who told them. Jesus called his hearers, and presumably also those of us who would read or hear his words in the future, to respect the requirement to make them our own, to allow them to speak that which is for us a particular truth or a precious insight. We must let each one who has ears to hear do the hearing and the understanding.

There is, however, a question that lies behind any consideration of these metaphors of the kingdom of heaven, a question which is very relevant in a book about the Christian doctrine of the hereafter. It centres on the very word 'heaven', as used in these instances. Was this 'kingdom', in the thought of Jesus, something simply to be worked out in the here and now, in Galilee and Judea, or did it involve something beyond earthly possibilities? Was it 'heaven' as we have come to understand it, or was it a vision of a renewed earth?

## As it is in heaven

Some of the best-known words of Jesus may throw light on this question. In the Lord's Prayer the second petition is this: 'Your kingdom come; your will be done on earth, as it is in heaven' (see Matthew 6:10). Those words combine two profound concepts. One is of 'heaven', where God's will is perfectly fulfilled, and one is of a renewed earth, where those same principles are worked out in daily life. When Jesus announced, at the very start of his public ministry, that the 'kingdom of God has come near' (Mark 1:15) or 'is at hand' (NRSV margin) he seems to be combining the two ideas. Heaven and earth come together in the arrival of the divine Son and Messiah.

In Hebrew, the language of the 'Old Testament' (as Christians call it), 'heaven' and 'sky' are the same word. God was 'up above' and there was little notion that human beings could join him there. The individual dead were consigned to 'the Pit', where they effectively ceased to exist. As the psalmist puts it:

> I am counted among those who go down to the Pit;
> I am like those who have no help,
> like those forsaken among the dead;
> like the slain that lie in the grave,
> like those whom you remember no more,
> for they are cut off from your hand. (Psalm 88:4–5)

It's hard to see in that picture even the faintest pre-echo of the later Jewish beliefs in the resurrection of the dead, much less the full-blown New Testament vision of the New Jerusalem.

The notion of a future life of fulfilment in 'heaven' is not present in the teaching of the first five books of the Bible (the Pentateuch) and was only articulated with the coming of the great prophets of Israel in or around the sixth century BC. There was no real perception of life beyond death until the time of the various Jewish exiles and then the conquest of biblical Israel, first by the Greeks and then the Romans. These events seemed to signal the end, or at least the postponement, of the vision of Israel as 'God's kingdom', the unique source of blessing to the nations of the world.

# A new vision of heaven

At the same time, the prophets of Israel began to speak of a more spiritual vision of the 'kingdom' for which the people had longed and prayed. This vision is the basis of the teaching of Jesus about the ultimate purpose of God, a redeemed humanity in a new environment. Within that vision came two new concepts, the resurrection of the dead (for example Daniel 12:2) and the 'kingdom of God [which] is within you', in the words of Jesus (Luke 17:21, KJV).

The first of these is the cause of the disputes recorded in the Gospels between Jesus, who believed in the resurrection, and the Sadducees, a sect who rejected the idea because it was not in 'the books of Moses' (the Pentateuch). There may be debate about what Jesus precisely believed on a number of issues of doctrine, but there can surely be no doubt at all that he robustly believed in the resurrection of the dead. 'He [God] is God not of the dead, but of the living' (Mark 12:27). This was his answer to the Sadducees' question about the resurrection of the dead—words echoed in Matthew and Luke. This was clearly a core truth of the message of Jesus. 'You are quite wrong,' he curtly told the Sadducees.

For the Christian, the most convincing evidence for life beyond this life is, quite simply, this clear and unequivocal endorsement of it by Jesus. If anyone knows, one might argue, the Son of God should. Of course, that is simply a circular argument for those who don't believe in his unique relationship with God. We shall, however, come later to other pieces of evidence which strongly point in the same direction.

The belief of Jesus in 'the resurrection of the dead' does not mean that he held a crudely literal view of it, rather like that suggested by the resurrection of the 'dry bones' in

Ezekiel 37. When the Sadducees asked him a trick question about marriage in heaven—who would be the husband of a woman who on earth had had seven husbands?—he ridiculed their question. They didn't understand the whole concept of heaven. 'Those who are considered worthy of… the resurrection' would be 'like angels in heaven'—in other words, spiritual beings not concerned with matters related only to earthly life and its arrangements (Luke 20:35; Mark 12:25).

That might lead us to ask, are we then like angels or spirits in 'heaven'? To most people the idea is not attractive—an eternity of existence as a wispy spook or a gleaming angel isn't quite what we had been led to expect. Neither, of course, is it what the New Testament asserts, and it falls far short of the glorious vision of the kingdom of heaven and the New Jerusalem which are the foundation concepts of the Christian 'heaven'. Jesus never offered any description of heaven nor any details about what it would be like, beyond one central truth. God, our heavenly Father, is there. That's what makes it heavenly. It is also what makes it essentially spiritual: 'God is spirit,' Jesus asserted (John 4:24) and therefore his kingdom, the kingdom of God, is spiritual.

To sound a note that will constantly ring from these pages, the real question is whether spiritual is superior to physical. We find that hard to accept, because we are physical beings and everything we enjoy flows from that physicality. Yet in the end we are faced with the inevitable end of that physicality. Death, in the Christian vision, is moving from the physical world of atoms and molecules into the spiritual world of God. When Paul writes at length on this, his whole argument is based on the superiority of the spiritual: 'So it is with the resurrection of the dead. What is sown is perishable, what is raised is imperishable. It is sown in dishonour, it is raised in glory. It is sown in weakness, it is raised in power. It is sown a physical body, it is raised a spiritual body' (1 Corinthians 15:42–44).

Jesus spoke of this spiritual kingdom almost entirely in metaphors, as we have seen. Most of them have a common theme: richness, growth, fulfilment, welcome, rejoicing. The angels in heaven celebrate each repentant sinner who thereby enters the kingdom (Luke 15:7). Like the good shepherd who finds the lost sheep, or the widow who finds her lost necklace coin, heaven is cause for joy. That it also involves judgement does not cast a shadow over the celebration, for in biblical thought judgement is not a bad thing but a good one. It brings conclusion, ties up loose ends, and unites justice and mercy. We shall return to the subject of judgement in a later chapter.

This chapter is about visions and metaphors, which are at the heart of biblical language about heaven. Unpacking them to uncover the profound imaginative insight that inhabits them is not easy for people immersed in a world of science, technology and factual reportage. It is interesting, though, to see the contemporary appeal of films and books that employ visionary images. Fantasy still fascinates modern people and they do not balk at the idea of 'interpreting' it. Visions, in the biblical sense, are 'revelation': pictures, images, dreamlike presentations of profound truths. Surely they still speak to the human imagination?

Metaphors are common enough in poetry, drama and even everyday speech. It should not be beyond everyday experience, then, to approach the metaphorical sayings of Jesus with the same tools as we employ day by day. Are we trying to be *too* 'holy' and missing the essentially simple thrust of the language of the Gospels? Profound imaginative insight inhabits these metaphors, but ordinary people understood them well enough 2000 years ago. We can't approach them like a train timetable or the instructions for a new microwave oven, but a little imagination can unlock a world of understanding. We may not be gardeners, but we know the basic principles of growth from a tiny seed to a plant, a bush or a steepling tree. We may not be traders in precious stones, but we can understand that there might be one so beautiful that it would be worth sacrificing everything else to own it. We may not be a child psychiatrist, but we know that the mind of a child has a glorious simplicity about it and a profound sense of dependence and trust. Those are the simple tools we need to bring to the metaphors.

The visions are different, because they are essentially using a literary form unfamiliar to many modern readers in order to express profound spiritual truths. They are the stuff of dreams, of fantasy, of horror and ecstasy. They often take us far beyond our comfort zone—think of the terrifying visions in Revelation. But, like most dreams, they do not end in horror but in heaven—equally vivid images of glory, beauty and fulfilment. There is perhaps some danger in dipping a toe into them. We need to plunge in and soak up the images—horror or ecstasy—while staying open to their spiritual significance. That may sometimes be very difficult to discern, but if we can 'interpret' Harry Potter and space fantasies it should not be beyond many younger readers today.

Many of the visions in the Bible are recorded by people recognised as 'seers' or prophets. A seer is, by definition, someone who 'sees', but sees further or more penetratingly than others. A prophet is someone who from a heightened state of spiritual awareness speaks out profound truth. Many of these visions have their origin in dreams—'night visions', as they are called in the book of Daniel. Dreams have an enormous role in the biblical story, both in the Hebrew scriptures and in the Christian ones. In our dreams we are, it seems, liberated to explore our subconscious mind. In that state of liberation from the everyday some people have received extraordinarily clear visions of truth and been able afterwards to record them. This is not necessarily true of all dreams, of course. Not every dreamlike premonition is a genuine warning, nor is every dreamlike wish-fulfilment a promise of future realisation.

It does seem true, however, that in our sleep, and perhaps especially in that half-conscious state between sleep and being fully awake, some receptive minds are particularly open to experience genuine God-given visions. The seer John, who recorded the astonishingly vivid visions of Revelation (the Apocalypse) says that he was on the island of Patmos 'in the spirit on the Lord's day' when they came to him (1:10). The disciples who reported the 'transfiguration' of Jesus on a mountaintop, along with visions of Moses and Elijah, were—the physician Luke tells us—'weighed down with sleep' (9:32). The book of Daniel is very explicit: 'Daniel had a dream and visions of his head as he lay in bed' (7:1). Not all visions are dreams, and certainly not all dreams are visions. The dreamlike quality of the visionary language of the Bible ought to warn readers not to try to apply it literally. We need to approach great visions with care, laying aside our 21st-century footwear and putting on heavenly sandals. This is truth indeed, but it is poetic truth, pictorial insight into deep things, human imagination at full stretch to describe the ineffable.

> *A man's reach should exceed his grasp,*
> *Or what's a heaven for?*
>
> Robert Browning (1812–89), *Andrea del Sarto*

# Chapter Two

## A place for you

> *To believe in heaven is not to run away from life; it is to run towards it.*
>
> Joseph D. Blinco (1912–68)

The previous chapter looked at the metaphors and visions which the New Testament tends to use when speaking of heaven. I have conceded that for many present-day people that is an unfamiliar approach (even though, as we have seen, both metaphorical and visionary language is constantly before us in books, plays, poetry and popular television series). The examples I have used so far have been taken either from what are called the 'synoptic' Gospels (Matthew, Mark and Luke, so called because they see things through the 'one eye'), or from the kind of dreamlike visions found in the book of Revelation.

There is, however, one very clear instance when the Fourth Gospel, John, records words Jesus spoke to his disciples on the night of his betrayal and the eve of his crucifixion. These words are not metaphorical or visionary, but sound like a fairly plain statement of fact—even if the facts are, in truth, mind-blowing. Here is the passage, from John's Gospel, chapter 14:

*'Do not let your hearts be troubled. Believe in God, believe also in me. In my Father's house there are many dwelling-places. If it were not so, would I have told you that I go to prepare a place for you? And if I go and prepare a place for you, I will come again and will take you to myself, so that where I am, there you may be also. And you know the way to the place where I am going.' Thomas said to him, 'Lord, we do not know where you are going. How can we know the way?' Jesus said to him, 'I am the way, and the truth, and the life. No one comes to the Father except through me.' (John 14:1–6)*

The great advantage of this passage is that it is entirely free of imagery. It simply tells it the way it is, or rather, the way Jesus wanted his friends to understand what was about to happen. It is the only instance in the Gospels of Jesus speaking about 'heaven' in an explanatory, rather than in a metaphorical or confrontational way. Of course, strictly speaking his subject was not 'heaven' but 'going to the Father'. There is no doubt, though, that heaven is where the Father is. That's common ground throughout the Hebrew and Christian scriptures. So we are entitled, it seems to me, to take this as a manifesto about the future that awaits the followers of Jesus, and that that is heaven.

There will be some, doubtless, who cavil about the fact that these words are in the Fourth Gospel, in which Jesus generally sounds very different from the teacher of the other Gospels. John's Gospel, while telling in substance the same story as the other three Gospels, gives its readers a different perspective on the prophet from Galilee. It is an intensely nuanced picture, clearly written or resourced by someone who knew him very well and was deeply devoted to him. Here is the story of the Son of God, to match the Synoptics' wonderfully earthy picture of the Son of Man. These are the words of Jesus of Nazareth, but they are spoken by a man who will not be that for much longer. The Son of Man is 'going to the Father'.

Mark's Gospel starts in the wilderness of Judea with John the Baptist. Matthew's Gospel starts with Abraham, the father of the nation of Israel. Luke begins with Adam, the founder of the human race. John starts even further back: 'In the beginning was the Word, and the Word was with God, and the Word was God.' It is like four different television reporters, each with a different remit from the producer, giving four equally convincing pictures of the same event but from different perspectives. John, a Gospel rooted in the long aftershock of the incarnation, cannot be accused of presenting a 'different' picture of Jesus. This, with the other Gospels, is the apostolic message. It was this that 'turned the world upside down' (see Acts 17:6). To quote the title of Richard Burridge's scholarly book on this subject, there are 'four Gospels but one Jesus'. Without the Jesus of the Fourth Gospel the picture is incomplete.

What we have in this passage is a series of clear statements about heaven. They centre on three nouns which are crucial to any understanding of the teaching of the New Testament about the 'hereafter': house, dwelling-places and place. The passage begins, however, with a moving call to faith. The disciples were not to be 'troubled in heart' at the thought of his death, which Jesus had just reminded them was imminent. Instead, they should remember that they believed in God, and 'believe also in me'. The heart of this word for believe is 'trust'. 'Trust God,' Jesus is saying, 'and trust me.' Through the two years or so of their discipleship, they had learnt that Jesus was an extraordinary leader, someone they could rely on, whether it was in a storm-tossed boat on Lake Galilee or facing crowds of people desperate for his healing touch. They were his disciples; he was their teacher. How would they manage without him? His simple, one-word answer was 'trust'.

## The Father's house

Jesus doesn't, however, leave it there. He was 'going to the Father', but that would not be the end of the journey, for him or for them. 'In my Father's house there are many dwelling-places.' Here is a new idea dropped into the situation. 'The Father's house' was a phrase commonly used among the Jews to describe the Temple—remember the boy Jesus chiding his parents for not realising that he would have been 'in the Father's house', the Temple, rather than the streets and markets of the city.

Here, however, Jesus is not using the word to describe an earthly building, however grand and sacred. 'House', even in English, can mean much more than a physical building. Houses are more about people than bricks. We have the 'house of Windsor', and at school many of us belonged to various 'houses'. This is a common meaning in the Greek of the New Testament, where a 'house' encompasses the idea of a family, a tribe (the 'house of Judah') or a community. This expands the idea far beyond a physical location. We might even say that 'in the future community of God' there will be many 'dwelling-places'.

## Dwelling-places

That brings us to the second significant noun, 'dwelling-place'. The Greek word (*monai*) covers an enormous diversity of residences. It certainly can mean 'house', in our modern sense, but it could equally mean 'stopping-place' (or, to be very vernacular, 'motel'). It is frequently used to describe any place where one stops to rest, as well as those places where we 'abide'. One feels that behind this whole passage the idea of travelling is constantly present. Jesus was on a journey to the Father. Soon the disciples would follow. Their destination would be 'the Father's house' and at the journey's end, or even perhaps on the way, there will be places to stop.

Indeed, Jesus places himself here in the role of the 'dragoman', the servant who went ahead of the first-century caravans of camels with their valuable cargo and their important passengers, to prepare each evening's place of rest. The dragoman would light a fire, prepare a meal, and see that tents and mattresses were ready, so that the weary travellers would be welcomed and provided for on their long and hot journey. All of that is surely implied in Jesus' promise that he was going to 'prepare a place for you'. The disciples' Rabbi-Messiah-Dragoman would be there to greet them and welcome them on their way to the Father's house.

## A place for you

That brings us to the word 'place': 'I am going to prepare a place.' Again, both in English and in Greek, the word can be used literally (of a specific geographical location) or of a social or metaphysical identification ('I know my place in society'). 'Place' is more than simply a physical location, a grid reference on a map. Indeed, possessing a 'place' of our own, a location that is familiar and where we feel 'at home', is one of the great gifts of a contented life. Here it is what Jesus promises his friends: 'I go to prepare a place for you.'

What that does not necessarily mean, however, is that 'the Father's house' or heaven has a geographical location. That is one of the concepts which has made modern people so sceptical about the whole idea of heaven. 'Where is it?' they ask. We've searched space, but no sign of it. Is there a vast acreage of real estate floating around somewhere in space, large enough to be the permanent dwelling-place of billions of people?

Even to ask the questions is to reduce the concept of heaven to a pointless dispute about impossibilities. As we shall see later, the clue to it all lies in the nature and being of God, not in a space-time concoction that owes more to old-fashioned science fiction than to the teaching of the New Testament. Heaven is a 'place' in the most profound and fundamental sense of the word: home, fulfilment, security, love. For such fulfilment, we really don't need pearly gates or golden streets or even the river of life (though they are rich in poetic and visionary meaning). We don't need to ask 'where' heaven is. Heaven is where God is. He is not somewhere 'in' his universe. It would be more accurate to say that the universe is 'in' him. It is quite natural that we humans tend to use earthly and space-time language in our thinking—how else could we take on board the complexities of existence in eternity? Yet in the end, surely, when (in

Paul's words) we 'see face to face' rather than 'dimly, in a mirror', what now seems beyond comprehension will be revealed as transparent, eternal truth. Meanwhile, we can trust where we can't understand. In the immortal words of the Beatles, 'All you need is love.' And God is love.

House, place, dwelling-places: key words of heaven. It is the Father's house, the kingdom of God, the community of his people. His Son Jesus 'prepares' the place which we shall share with him.

From those three words—house, dwelling-place, place—we now move on to three more, this time as an answer to the entirely reasonable question, 'What is the way to this desirable place?' It was Thomas, the statutory sceptic of the apostolic band, who queried the claim by Jesus that they already knew 'the way to the place where I am going'. Thomas' challenge produced the final one of the famous 'I am' sayings of Jesus in this Gospel: 'I am the way, and the truth, and the life' (John 14:6). The words themselves are deceptively simple. We use them regularly in everyday speech. Yet they enshrine the most profound insights into the mystery of the incarnation and of the unique role of the Son of God in our journey to the kingdom of heaven.

Jesus is 'the way'—presumably, in context, the way to the Father. The phrase is terse. I realise it is a favourite trick of preachers to build a whole argument on what it *doesn't* say, but in this case what he doesn't say is very significant. Jesus is the way. It isn't that he shows us the way, or is a signpost directing us to God (though both statements are true to his teaching). It isn't that following his commandments will bring us to the Father (though he says as much later in this discourse). He *is* the way—that's to say, the pathway, the road to the Father.

Many years ago, working on a radio broadcast from Jerusalem, a colleague who needed to find the way to the Damascus Gate asked an Arab man in the street to tell him how to find it. 'I am the way,' he said, taking my friend's arm and walking with him to the gate. At this point, it wasn't instruction or advice the disciples needed, but the promise of Jesus to be with them through the whole process of discovery—in fact, like my colleague's helper, to take them there. Later, after his resurrection, Jesus would assure them that he would be with them 'always, to the end of the age' (Matthew 28:20). Knox's Catholic translation of Matthew renders the word 'always' in its absolutely literal meaning: 'all roads'.

The poet Alice Meynell (1847–1922), in a sensitive poem 'I am the way' about this saying of Jesus, picks up this theme very powerfully.

> *Thou art the Way.*
> *Hadst Thou been nothing but the goal*
> *I cannot say*
> *If Thou hadst ever met my soul.*

However, she ends the poem with a simple focus on the whole meaning of 'way':

> *I'll not reproach*
> *The road that winds, my feet that err.*
> *Access, Approach*
> *Art Thou, Time, Way and Wayfarer.*

I think this captures very beautifully the various ways in which we use the word 'way': time, access, approach, wayfarer. From 'What is the way to boil an egg?' to 'How can I get into university?' that little three-lettered word is a common element. It seems to me that in Christian belief Jesus fulfils all of those definitions: how to, where, access, by what means. 'Going to the Father' simply makes no sense without a guide and a means of access, let alone a companion on the journey.

The one who is the 'way' is also the 'truth'. The way to God, Jesus, is also the truth about God, or perhaps more precisely the truth *of* God. All through the ages of human history people have asked 'What is God like?' Here is the claim, as Michael Ramsey once memorably put it: 'God is Christ-like, and Christ is God-like.' Or, as Jesus goes on to say here: 'Whoever has seen me has seen the Father' (John 14:9). It is a bold—indeed, staggering—claim, the ultimate either in insane delusion or blatant blasphemy if not true. Jesus sits among his friends and coolly says, 'If you want to know what the Father is like, look at me.' There are two astonishing things about the claim: that the teacher from Nazareth dared to make it, and that his hearers, who had watched him and lived with him for several years, believed it.

The 'truth' here is not a doctrinal assertion, but a disclosure of a revelation. Jesus was not saying that he was a human compendium of facts about God, but that by the miracle of the incarnation ('Do you not believe that I am in the Father and the Father is in me?' John 14:10) he provided a unique insight into what the Creator himself is like. 'No one has ever seen God. It is God the only Son, who is close to the

Father's heart, who has made him known' (John 1:18). If the disciples, and we in our turn, are 'going to the Father', it is reassuring to know the nature and character of the One towards whom we are travelling and in whose 'house' we shall eventually find a dwelling-place.

'I am the way, and the truth...' but also 'the life'. Jesus is the way to God and the truth of God, and he is also the life of God. That is probably a more elusive concept. In the opening verses of John's Gospel it is said of Jesus, 'In him was life, and the life was the light of all people' (v. 4). That is obviously saying much more than that he was 'alive'. It implies that he is a source of life for people—that in him the divine life, the life of the Creator himself, was not just present but available. 'Because I live, you also will live,' Jesus once said (John 14:19). Through him the life of God, divine life, became available to his human creatures. 'I have come,' said Jesus on yet another occasion, 'that they may have life, and have it to the full' (John 10:10, NJB).

It's worth remembering that all of this was said in the context of a dialogue about 'going to the Father'. It is, in other words, about heaven, the 'place' that Jesus was going to prepare for his friends, the 'house' that contains 'many dwelling-places'. Jesus is not here telling his friends what heaven is like, but how to get there. He is the 'way', but they would also find in their relationship with him all the truth that they needed to know on the journey, and all the spiritual energy (the 'life') that it would demand. The Father is heaven, and heaven is the Father—and the way there is not a set of theological propositions but the companionship of the Father's Son.

# What about hell?

That, so far as this book is concerned, is a summary of what the Bible, and especially the New Testament, has to say about heaven. But what, one might ask, about hell? Isn't that also an essential part of what people have understood as the teaching of the Christian Church about the hereafter? It certainly is, in common usage. The 'good' go to heaven and the 'evil' go to hell. Over the centuries the threat of eternal punishment in the latter has probably outweighed in many people's minds the promise of eternal bliss in the former.

That is, of course, a crude and misleading interpretation of the Bible's teaching on the subject. The confusion can be illustrated by the fact that the English word 'hell' is commonly used to translate the Hebrew word *sheol*, the Aramaic word (the language of Jesus) *gehenna* and the Greek word *hades*. In ordinary English speech 'hell' is a place of torment, especially by fire—the final destination of the irredeemably wicked. *Sheol* and *hades* have no connotation of judgement or punishment. They are, quite simply, the 'abode of the dead'. The only one of the three words applied in the Bible to judgement and punishment is *gehenna*, which Jesus used to describe a place of final purging of wickedness. 'Gehenna' was in fact an actual location, a valley outside Jerusalem where, according to a twelfth-century rabbi, the city's rubbish was consumed in a continuously burning fire.

We are all familiar with the need to dispose of rubbish and refuse. Nowadays we recycle a lot of it (an interesting thought!), but still we need to put out things that if left alone would endanger health or pollute the environment. Fire cleanses. It did in the first century, and it still does. The endless fires of Gehenna kept Jerusalem free from disease and decay. They made a telling image of God's ultimate purpose for the 'new' Jerusalem: a place free from corruption, decay and evil—in the words of Revelation, a place where 'righteousness' dwells.

The nearest thing in the Bible to the traditional images of hell—sulphurous fire, demons, terror—is the 'lake that burns with fire' or 'second death' which is described in the final visions of Revelation (21:8). It stands in sharp contrast to the vision of the New Jerusalem which immediately precedes it, where death, mourning, crying and pain will be no more (21:4). It is stating the obvious to observe that heaven would not be heaven if it housed evil and wickedness. In that case we would be back to where we are now. The judgement and removal of evil from the creation is the great theme of the strange visions of Revelation, but so is the constant offer of the 'water of life'. The Lamb of God 'who takes away the sin of the world' is continually present in the visions, alongside the 'One who sits on the throne': ultimate mercy alongside ultimate judgement. Indeed, it is the Saviour of the world who has been appointed by the Father to be its Judge. I think most of us would settle for being judged by the one who has done most to secure our forgiveness.

The truth is that 'heaven' and 'hell' are words that have been used throughout human history to describe the ultimately indescribable. They take us beyond the reach of human reason and experience into a mode of being—free from time and space—which stretches our imaginations to breaking point. No wonder the biblical revelation prefers metaphor and vision, inviting us to trust the Creator to know best what the fulfilling of his purpose will mean for both the creation and its creatures.

# Chapter Three

## Intimations of immortality

> *Earth has no sorrow that heaven cannot heal.*
>
> Thomas Moore (1779–1852),
> 'Come, Ye Disconsolate'

Over the years I have asked hundreds of bereaved people—often months after the event, even years—whether they feel as though their loved one has ceased to exist. So far, I have never had the answer 'Yes'. I notice that this feeling is not confined to my contacts. Robert Peston, the former BBC economics correspondent, was interviewed a year after the death of his wife, a young woman in her forties. Asked about how he thought about her now, he replied that although he was not conventionally religious, he had a strong feeling that she was still 'there'.

Forty years ago a Welsh GP, Dewi Rees, conducted a major piece of research into this experience. It began as his MD thesis for the University of London, supervised by a senior psychiatrist appointed by the university. Dr Rees sought the experience of a very large number of bereaved people in the wide area of mid-Wales covered by his practice. He conducted one-to-one interviews with 293 respondents, about a quarter of them men. His findings were eventually published in 1971 in the *British Medical Journal*, volume 4, under the title 'The Hallucinations of Widowhood', and more recently he has expanded on them in a book, *Pointers to Eternity* (Y Lofla, 2010).

His findings attracted national and international attention, an interest pursued by a number of academic researchers overseas, and particularly in the USA. To his surprise he found that similar pieces of research undertaken in several different countries and in other parts of Britain following the publication of his paper produced almost identical results. About half of the bereaved people interviewed in all of these samples, covering in all many hundreds of people, said that they had had a specific experience relating to their loved one. This sometimes took the form of a spoken word, or a sense of presence, or a visual experience or even occasionally a touch. Gender made no difference. The experiences were the same in nature and frequency whatever the identity of those involved. All but a tiny minority (6 per cent) found the experience positive rather than disturbing.

A few days after my wife Christine died in 2001 I had a similar experience—not of a word or a touch but of an inexplicable event—which assured me that she was happy and I was not to grieve for her. This was witnessed by the visiting Macmillan bereavement counsellor. The counsellor was talking about possible books that might help my grandchildren to cope with Grandma's death. She was holding one in her hand, 'a Christian book' she said, slightly apologetically (she didn't know I was a priest!), which children often enjoyed. It was about a larva which left the others in the pool to rise into the sky as a dragonfly. At that moment something landed on the book. 'What's that?' I asked. She looked shocked. 'It's a dragonfly!' she said. This happened on a cool day in early May, with all the windows shut. I had never seen a dragonfly anywhere near the house before, nor have I subsequently. By nature I am a typically sceptical journalist, yet even I could not deny that this seemed to be some kind of a sign, an intentional message to me. Rightly or wrongly, I took it as such, and was relieved to discover from Dewi Rees' research that such events were not at all unusual—though not often in so dramatic a form.

In a more recent book, *Daniel, My Son* (Splendid Publications, 2015), a father, David Thomas, writes movingly of the death of his brilliant young son of bone cancer. A few months after his death, the author was staying the night alone in a hotel and casually switched on the television. The programme that came on was *University Challenge*, and soon a question came up about hymn tunes. Of the four hymn tunes played, three were of hymns sung at Daniel's funeral. That was surprising enough, but then Mr Thomas realised that the college attempting the answers was Daniel's old college, Magdalen, Oxford. Being of a statistical frame of mind, he began to work out the odds, factoring in the further piece of evidence, provided by the BBC, that this was the first time since 1994 that there had been a question about hymn tunes. He calculated that the likelihood of this happening by chance was between five million and ten million to one. As he says in his book, 'sadly none of this proves that Daniel still exists', but two other similar experiences, one involving Daniel's mother, and many stories he has heard from bereaved parents of other sarcoma victims, do at the least bear out the findings of the research by Dewi Rees.

I'm not sure what these experiences taken as a whole actually tell us about a putative 'hereafter', though mine, for example, is one that it's hard to explain in other terms. For the most part, it seems to me, they are testimonies of the enduring power of love. When Robert Peston, in the newspaper interview I quoted earlier, was asked if he had any explanation of his 'feeling' that his late wife was still with him, his eventual reply was one word, 'love'. Paul says that 'love never ends' (1 Corinthians 13:8). Indeed, love 'abides', or 'lasts for ever' (see v. 13). For the Christian, that is not surprising, because 'God is love' (1 John 4:8), and God is, by very definition, eternal.

If love is the key to these bereavement experiences, as I suspect it is, it would be a wrong conclusion to assume that that is *all* it is. It may well be that human love at its best is so powerful and inextinguishable a force that its echo, as it were, could produce feelings and sensual experiences like those described by so many bereaved people. But not surely, I would have to add, to embody itself as an actual dragonfly landing on an actual book in the presence of witnesses.

However, it would be equally wrong to assume that the occasional apparently inexplicable experience 'proves' life after death. Such experiences are, as Rees' book is titled, 'pointers' rather than conclusive evidence. What they are 'proof' of, in fact, is the remarkable durability of truly loving relationships. That is one of the 'pointers' and not a minimal one. After all, in Christian belief the very Godhead is a relationship of love. The Holy Trinity is held together, we are told, by love (John 17:23).

# Experiences and appearances

*Pointers to Eternity* elicited, among many responses, a debate about the difference between experiences and appearances. Could it be, for instance, that the biblical accounts of the appearances of Jesus to his followers after his crucifixion were, in fact, experiences of the kind the book describes? After all, the title of Rees' original paper for the British Medical Association was 'Hallucinations of Widowhood', though later he very deliberately rejected the word 'hallucination' as a description of the experiences he recorded. Nevertheless, human history is replete with examples of hallucinations—visionary experiences which are intensely real to those who see them, but generally unconvincing for everyone else. Most ghost stories seem to fall into that category. Could it be that the first disciples, in the aftermath of the hideous events of the crucifixion, and full of profound affection for the Leader they had lost, may have experienced what one could call hallucinations?

This was the subject of a 1976 article entitled 'The Resurrection and Bereavement Experiences' written by the Roman Catholic biblical scholar Fr Gerald O'Collins SJ in the *Irish Theological Quarterly* (vol. 76, no. 3, pp. 224–237). He was concerned that Rees' research might lead people to suppose that the appearances of Jesus recorded in the Gospels after his death might be no more than similar experiences born of intense personal loss. He and Rees exchanged papers, and both came to the conclusion that the biblical appearances were of a different category from the recorded experiences of the bereaved.

# The resurrection of Jesus

It seems to me worth looking into the difference in nature of the two things, because there is enough overlap to confuse the issue. After all, the resurrection of Jesus is fundamental, in Christian terms, to an understanding of life after death, 'that undiscovered country from whose bourn no traveller returns', as Hamlet puts it. Well, in Christian belief one Traveller *has* returned, and even talked about it (though, interestingly, not much, and not at all in descriptive terms). The resurrection of Jesus is a cornerstone of the traditional Christian case, and rightly so.

The earliest account of it is not in the Gospels, but in Paul's letter to the church at Corinth, probably written about AD55, a mere 20 or so years after the crucifixion of Jesus. Paul sets out very clearly what he was taught when he was prepared for baptism around AD36—two or three years after that first Easter weekend and while its consequences were still fresh in people's minds. Here is what he wrote:

> *For I handed on to you as of first importance what I in turn had received: that Christ died for our sins in accordance with the scriptures, and that he was buried, and that he was raised on the third day in accordance with the scriptures, and that he appeared to Cephas, then to the twelve. Then he appeared to more than five hundred brothers and sisters*

*at one time, most of whom are still alive, though some have*
*died. Then he appeared to James, then to all the apostles.*
*(1 Corinthians 15:3–7)*

This is, as I say, the earliest account we have of the resurrection of Jesus. It bears the hallmarks of a known narrative—an early creedal confession, possibly—but also of someone dictating his words to a scribe. There are obvious repetitions: the 'twelve' were the apostles, and included others he names, notably Cephas (Peter), and James, who were the recognised leaders of the Church at that time. Twice his statement asserts that this happened 'in accordance with the scriptures'; that is, foretold by the prophets of Israel. On the other hand, he doesn't mention the women, who by the unanimous testimony of the Gospels were the first witnesses of the empty tomb, or Mary Magdalene, the very first person to see the risen Christ. The Gospels do not mention an appearance to 500 people at once, which would be a very significant part of the evidence for the resurrection—especially the claim that many of them were still alive 33 years or so after the appearance.

This shows, then, how difficult it is to put together a single, coherent account of the resurrection of Jesus. When we turn to the Gospels, we find the same situation. Apart from Mark, whose truncated Gospel records no appearances of Jesus (while clearly asserting that he had risen), they record many such appearances, some to individuals, like the couple on the road to Emmaus (Luke 24:13–35), and Peter and his companions on the lake (John 21). Others were to larger groups of people: the disciples in the upper room (John

20:19) and on the mount of the ascension (Luke 24:50–52; Acts 1:6–11). The appearances were all transient or at least temporary, in widely differing geographical locations, and twice in locked and bolted rooms. Jesus 'appeared', and then withdrew from people's sight.

The witnesses all attest that it was undoubtedly Jesus they encountered, though on several occasions they recorded that at first they didn't recognise him (for example, John 20:14; Luke 24:15–16). What they saw was not, they were clear, a 'ghost', but equally clearly it was not an ordinary flesh-and-blood person—otherwise, how could they account for the appearing and disappearing? He was, in other words, Jesus their Lord and teacher—they were prepared to die for that belief (and many of them did). But he was not Jesus as they had known him on the dusty lanes of Galilee or the crowded streets of Jerusalem.

I believe there is a key that unlocks the mystery of the resurrection of Jesus, and of the resurrection which the Christian creeds speak of. It is found in the same chapter of Paul's first letter to the Corinthians as the earlier excerpt. It is, I think, a crucial key to understanding, but it is one many Christians seem to be unwilling to turn. It is found in a passage I quoted earlier, a series of repeated assertions about resurrection: 'So it is with the resurrection of the dead. What is sown is perishable, what is raised is imperishable… It is sown in weakness, it is raised in power. It is sown a physical body, it is raised a spiritual body' (1 Corinthians 15:42–44).

Paul is answering an oratorical question: 'How are the dead raised?' The central and repeated point he makes in answer is that they are raised 'spiritually'. In case one imagines that his is simply a lone voice in the early Church and the New Testament, his point is made more briefly but equally clearly by the apostle Peter: 'Christ... was put to death in the flesh, but made alive in the spirit' (1 Peter 3:18). Whatever resurrection is, whether of Jesus or of people today, it is emphatically not a physical restoration of the body. 'Flesh and blood cannot inherit the kingdom of God,' says Paul (1 Corinthians 15:50).

As I said earlier, many people are unhappy about this assertion. They think that 'raised in the spirit' means that we shall be wispy ghosts in heaven, and that is not an attractive idea. On the whole, we rather like our bodies (when they are functioning properly), and we cannot imagine being human without them—and it is as humans, as 'people', not spectres, that we expect to enjoy eternal life. A closer reading of Paul's words in the letter to the Corinthians, however, shows that he is not remotely suggesting that in the resurrection life people will be ghosts. I suspect the very idea would have reduced him to eloquent fury. The risen spirit (whether of Jesus or of you and me) will have a 'body' in which to express itself, but it won't be this one, or anything else that would wear out, decay or perish. That is the heart of his argument.

When we apply that insight—'turn that key'—to the question of the Gospel accounts of the resurrection of Jesus, we shall find that many of the difficulties disappear. When the women came to the empty tomb on Easter morning, the 'young man dressed in a white robe' said to them, 'You are looking for Jesus of Nazareth, who was crucified. He has been raised; he is not here' (Mark 16:6). Jesus of

Nazareth, the son of the village carpenter, was not there, or, in a sense, anywhere else. The 'incarnation' was over. They would meet the risen Messiah, but they would not ever again see the carpenter's son. 'He has been raised'—and in that resurrection transformed from a first-century Jewish man into a citizen of his Father's kingdom of heaven. And that, says Paul, is the pattern for all our resurrections. It was, as the disciples recorded in their bewilderment and confusion, the same Jesus who appeared to them, but different: not less, but more—no longer limited by the restrictions of physicality, of space and time, but gloriously, powerfully, *spiritual*.

We may find it hard to appreciate that this is to be more, not less, alive. We are immersed in an intensely physical world, where things are held together by time and space. That hesitancy is understandable, and probably doesn't matter provided we are willing to accept that there might be—indeed there is—an infinitely better way of 'being' than what we have known during our lives on earth. It is a way of being which mirrors the very nature of God himself, as we shall see later. We, who are made in his 'image', will one day share his eternal being, freed from the limitations of the created universe to be with its Creator. That is the plain but staggering implication of the phrase 'eternal life'—not just life that lasts for ever, but life 'in all its fullness' (John 10:10, NJB).

## Resurrection and heaven

This book is about an eventual destiny for human beings, a place we have called 'heaven'. As we have seen, most of what the Bible has to say about it is metaphor or vision, both of which demand profound reflection and interpretation. However, as we have also seen, there has been one person who, in the language of the New Testament, had 'come from God and was going to God' (John 13:3), Jesus. That is why his death and resurrection are so central to the Christian understanding of heaven and the hereafter. He died and was buried. On the third day after his death he 'appeared' to a number of his friends, and continued to do so for several weeks, until the appearances ceased: he had finally 'gone to God'.

What is in a way frustrating is that we have no record of anything the risen Jesus said about where he had been, and (after his resurrection) nothing about where he was going except 'to the Father' (John 20:17). He had a different agenda, which concerned the task he was leaving his followers to fulfil. I say his silence is 'in a way' frustrating because, in truth, whatever he may have told them would have been utterly beyond their comprehension. He had told them, as we have seen, that he was going to prepare a 'place' for them where they would be with him, and that this place involved 'coming to the Father'. Beyond that, they and we are left to wonder at the implications of his words. What the risen Jesus had promised was 'eternal life', something that he had often talked about and was for all those who trusted him. Now, in the 40 days or so of his resurrection appearances, the disciples met and talked with a man they had known well, and whose death they had mourned, showing them in his own person what 'eternal life' is.

That is why the resurrection appearances of Jesus are so important in any consideration of the meaning of eternal life—the life Jesus promised to his followers. Here it was before them—but they struggled to capture in words the mystery of the transformation of Jesus of Nazareth into the risen Christ.

This seems, then, to be a good point at which to try to summarise what the Gospel writers, reflecting the experience of those first witnesses, tell us about the risen Christ. I have tried to summarise it under headings, but these are elusive truths and can't comfortably be tucked away in succinct propositions!

- All the witnesses were eventually in no doubt that they had met Jesus—the Jesus they knew, who was their teacher and friend. Those who were convinced included some who doubted at first (Matthew 28:17) and one (Thomas) who demanded proof, which he was offered (John 20:24–28).
- On several occasions, as we have seen, the disciples failed at first to recognise Jesus. This suggests either that they were completely overwhelmed by the experience, or that in some way Jesus had 'changed'.
- They were persuaded that the person they had encountered was not a 'ghost' or apparition (Luke 24:37–39).
- There is some implication that the risen Christ was not to be touched (John 20:17), though Thomas was invited to do so—but apparently didn't (John 20:27–28), and Matthew says that on the first Easter morning on their way from the empty tomb the disciples met Jesus and 'took hold of his feet' to worship him (Matthew 28:9).
- The resurrection was clearly a spiritual event, though

in a physical setting. The resurrection body of Jesus was obviously human (that is, he was identifiably a man), but yet it could pass through locked doors and disappear and reappear in places far apart.

• On several occasions the disciples recognised Jesus not by his physical appearance but by some typical act or gesture (see, for example, Luke 24:35; John 20:16).

• The risen Christ exhibited a full range of human emotions: love and affection, practical thoughtfulness and even indignation (see, for example, John 20:14–16; 21:9–10; Luke 24:25).

These conclusions suggest that the resurrection of Jesus as recorded in the Gospel accounts presents him as both the same person and yet 'different'. The differences seem to support Paul's claims in his first letter to the Corinthians that resurrection involves a fundamental change from physical to spiritual, with essential humanity now expressed in a new, resurrection body. 'God gives it [the 'body that is sown'] a body as he has chosen, and to each kind of seed its own body' (15:38). So, as the creeds affirm, we can believe in 'the resurrection of the body', but a body transformed from the physical (mortal, perishable, says Paul) to the spiritual (immortal, imperishable).

Taken together, the Gospel accounts of the resurrection appearances might seem imprecise and vague, even contradictory. It is true that it is impossible to harmonise some of the details—at what time did the women come to the tomb on Easter morning: 'while it was still dark' (John 20:1) or 'when the sun had risen' (Mark 16:2)? However, as a retired superintendent of police pointed out to a Bible study group in my parish long ago: 'Every detective knows that identical stories equal collusion.' It is, I feel, impossible to read these accounts without sensing the ground of truth in them, however much they may sometimes seem to be confused about details. The Gospel writers are gathering together material from many sources, mostly based on the oral transmission of evidence, some 40 years or so after the events. That is why Paul's brief report of what he had been taught as a candidate for baptism probably no more than three or four years after the crucifixion is so important as a touchstone of authenticity. Nevertheless, as he claims, eyewitnesses of the resurrection appearances were probably still alive when the earlier Gospels were written, and one of the Gospels, at least, bears the name of a primary witness, John, even if the book itself did not come into circulation until most if not all of the witnesses were dead.

Anyone reading the Gospel accounts closely will have questions to ask—ones which cannot, by their very nature, be answered today. The risen Jesus presumably wore clothes: where did they come from, or go to? On a couple of occasions the witnesses claim that he ate food. What (not to be too crudely functional) happened to it? And the body of Jesus of Nazareth which was laid in the sealed tomb but was conspicuously absent on Sunday morning: what happened to it? Did it dematerialise? Was it instantly transformed into a resurrection body, leaving no trace of his flesh and blood? Was it that, in the darkness of the tomb and in the space of an instant, the process which slowly reduces human bodies to dust and finally nothing occurred, and the transformation to resurrection took place 'in the twinkling of an eye' (1 Corinthians 15:52)?

As I say, there is no answer to these questions, nor could there be. What we do know, from the biblical evidence, is that the disciples, honest men and women, met with someone whom they recognised as Jesus. That recognition was so strong that their testimony, unlikely as it was, eventually brought into being the Christian Church. The Roman authorities, with every incentive to do so, given the rapid growth of the Christian sect in their midst, proved singularly helpless to disprove their claims. Eventually, of course, the religion that was based on the resurrection of Jesus from the dead became the religion of the Roman Empire.

It is also significant that the Jewish authorities, similarly anxious to dismiss this new sect in their community, could not effectively counter the believers' testimony. A new movement of enormous energy and profound conviction came into being based on one single defining claim: Jesus, the prophet from Nazareth, rose from the dead.

The significance of that in any consideration of heaven and the hereafter is that the man who was raised from death was the same one who had claimed that 'eternal life' was available through him. The resurrection was the way Jesus resumed his heavenly role and provides the model of all our resurrections. Heaven—'coming to the Father'—involves the transformation of the body (as it did for Jesus). Our present flesh and blood is well enough suited to life on this planet, in our known environment of time and space, but the kingdom of heaven requires something altogether new. According to Paul, 'we will all be changed, in a moment, in the twinkling of an eye, at the last trumpet' (1 Corinthians 15:51–52). Only then, he argues, when 'this mortal body puts on immortality', will death be 'swallowed up in victory' (15:54).

That, in a few sentences, is why the resurrection of Jesus, and the resurrection which he promised to forgiven sinners, is absolutely central to what we believe about heaven.

# Chapter Four

## Eternal life

> *The main object of religion is not to get a man into heaven, but to get heaven into a man.*
>
> Thomas Hardy (1840–1928)

'God so loved the world that he gave his only Son, so that everyone who believes in him may not perish but may have eternal life'—the words from John's Gospel must be some of the best known in the whole Bible (3:16). The trouble is that the Greek word *aionios*—eternal, indeterminate as to duration—is sometimes translated as 'everlasting'. That implies 'lasting for ever and ever', whereas 'eternal' can be taken to mean 'valid for all time', without any implication of duration. Older readers will remember the prayers that ended 'for ever and ever, Amen'. That phrase actually translates a Latin one that means, literally, 'world of worlds'. That is a bit different from 'for ever and ever'!

This is not, however, an argument about translation, because there is no word in our language that fully expresses what the Christian faith means by 'eternal'. God is eternal. That is the foundational belief, not solely of Christianity, but also of Judaism and Islam, and possibly other faiths. If he is *not* eternal, if he is subject to the passing of time, growing old, or changing with the epochs of human history, then he is not the God of the Bible, who simply and categorically *exists.*

The story in Exodus (ch. 3) of Moses at the burning bush was possibly a turning point in the human understanding of God. Until then, certainly in the records we have, 'god' generally referred to a being of power, possibly the creator of the world, but more importantly the god of a nation or tribe. The gods were hills or mountains, sun or moon, stone effigies or wooden carvings. Sometimes they were simply superhumans, like the gods and goddesses of Greek mythology—hunters, warriors, lovers, exhibiting the full range of human emotion, including anger and frustration. The Hebrew scriptures offered a more sophisticated vision of God. In the early books of the Bible one editorial 'strand' calls him by the sacred name Yahweh, yet he was sometimes depicted as acting rather like those 'gods' of the nations. In the Garden of Eden, for instance, he took a walk in the garden 'at the time of the evening breeze' (Genesis 3:8).

At the burning bush, however, Moses learned that the God of his ancestors, the One who had called Abraham from Ur to Canaan in search of the Unknown, was radically different. The God who spoke to Moses on that day was awesome ('Remove the sandals from your feet,' Moses was told, 'for… you are standing [on] holy ground') and at the same time compassionate ('I have observed the misery of my people… I have heard their cry'). When asked by Moses to tell him his name, he replied, 'I AM WHO I AM… This is my name… for all generations' (Exodus 3:5–7, 14–15).

'I AM' is the nearest one can get to translating the revealed Holy Name of God, Yahweh. The title is probably connected to the Hebrew verb 'to be' (*hwh*). Although the name Yahweh occurs almost 6000 times in the Hebrew scriptures, readers won't find it in most English translations of the Bible (the Jerusalem Bible is the exception). Whenever the Holy name occurs, it is printed in most of our Bibles simply as 'the LORD', the capital letters indicating that they are representing a name so holy that it should not be written out. Many of us are familiar with it in abbreviated forms, such as the '*ya*' in 'hallelujah' ('praise Yahweh').

This is not simply of scholarly importance. How we think of God shapes how we think about faith, discipleship, prayer and—in the case we are considering—heaven and eternity. The most important key to understanding what heaven might be like is to ask ourselves what God is like, because, as Jesus said, it is 'God's house'. Heaven is being with God, and God being with us. If we get that clear, most of the other questions we might raise become secondary.

However, that makes the nature of the God who is at the heart of heaven very important. What does it mean to say that God is 'Yahweh', I AM? The divine name he revealed to Moses (though, as we have said, the writers of earlier books of the Bible had used it) means that the God worshipped by the descendants of Abraham was not a tribal deity. He was intrinsically different from the gods of the other nations. He could not be confined to territorial limits. He was not simply someone who could 'do things for them' or bless their crops. He is (and the verb is crucial) the God of eternity, with no beginning and no end, the One who simply *exists*.Think of God as 'The Existing One' and I reckon you get very near to the profound meaning of his name.

So the life of God, Yahweh, is eternal. He is not part of time (or space, for that matter), because both are by-products of his creation. God is the Existing One, and all that exists does so because of him. That is (as a teenager might say) 'awesome'. It is beyond our imagining, but then so is the vastness of the universe, the depths of time, the astonishing order and consequence of the creation. Cosmologists speculate whether the universe itself might be infinite, without beginning or end. If so, whatever brought it into being (unless it came from nothing and nowhere) must be infinite. Christians can take comfort from the vision at the burning bush. The One we worship is infinite. Long before scientific theories of cosmology existed, indeed before anything existed, the God of the eternal present tense existed.

Heaven, Jesus said, is 'coming to the Father'. It is also, in an important sense, the Father coming to us (see John 14:6; Revelation 21:3–4). In an astonishing visionary passage the apostle Paul sees a time when everything in heaven and earth shall be one, as with Christ we are caught up into the splendour of God (1 Corinthians 15:28). That expresses for me the essence of heaven. Our destiny, fulfilling the Creator's purpose, is not only to share his kingdom but to share his life. In that case, we may assume that life in his kingdom is eternal, like his own—not simply 'going on for ever and ever', but sharing in the life of the Existing One.

The thought itself is mind-blowing, of course. But at least it renders irrelevant several of the 'most frequently asked questions' about heaven. What age will we be there? Will babies who die remain infants for all eternity? Will I still have my dodgy hips or my fading eyesight? Might we not get bored, as millennia follow millennia? Where there is no passage of time, there is by definition no 'age', no re-birth certificate, no possibility of tedium. In heaven we shall be alive in the way that God is alive, fully, splendidly, gloriously, satisfyingly. To take a trivial example, I remember as a 16-year-old sitting in the Royal Albert Hall and hearing the slow movement of Beethoven's Seventh Symphony for the first time. I was overwhelmed by its beauty and its sadness. Many of us have experienced moments in life when that is how we have felt. We say it was as though time stood still. Such human experiences are fleeting, however, as the world of time and events returns to cast its inevitable shadow. But at least we can use such memories as foretastes of the glory that is to come. It would be blasphemous, surely, to think that the kingdom of heaven will be disappointing!

In case anyone thinks that this is some newfangled interpretation of the Bible and the nature of God, I would like to end this chapter with the last verse of one of my favourite hymns, 'How shall I sing that majesty'. It dates from the 17th century, so it's hardly 'newfangled', and because it can use the power of image and metaphor, it says what I have tried to say with sharper focus. The whole concept of infinity and eternity is beyond rational human thought, but not the imagination of the poet. The hymn writer was John Mason (c. 1646–94), and this is the hymn's last verse:

*How great a Being, Lord, is thine,*
*Which doth all being keep!*
*Thy knowledge is the only line*
*To sound so vast a deep.*
*Thou art a sea without a shore,*
*a sun without a sphere;*
*Thy time is now and evermore,*
*Thy place is everywhere.*

---

**The capital of heaven is the heart in which Jesus Christ is enthroned as king.**

Sadhu Sundar Singh (1889–1929)

# Chapter Five

## Judgement

> *All the way to heaven is heaven.*
>
> St Catherine of Siena (1347–80)

If you asked a hundred people in the street what Christians believe happens after death, I suspect most of them would say something like 'God decides whether you go to heaven or hell.' That is how the message has come to them, through a garbled version of scripture, art and works like Dante's 'Inferno'. Many medieval churches still offer murals showing the good people flying up to heaven with blissful looks on their faces and the wicked sinners being prodded into the fiery furnace by the guardians of the inferno. I remember seeing in Pisa, in the chapel next to the famous Leaning Tower, a terrifyingly graphic painting of precisely that scene.

It offers, in fact, a caricature of the biblical vision of judgement. It has enough truth to perpetuate the idea, but not enough to make it remotely consistent with the Bible's profound vision of the fulfilment of God's ultimate purpose in the salvation of the world. Here is how the writer of the letter to the Hebrews expressed it: 'And just as it is appointed for mortals to die once, and after that the judgment, so Christ, having been offered once to bear the sins of many, will appear a second time, not to deal with sin, but to save those who are eagerly waiting for him' (9:27–28).

Judgement is a vital element in the story of the Bible, because God is supremely the 'Judge of all the earth'. Time and again the Hebrew scriptures remind us that he 'judges the world with equity', that 'the Judge of all the earth does what is right'. It is a great reassurance for the people of earth that they do not live in a lawless moral chaos, but that over everything—every evil scheme, every act of human wickedness—God's justice and judgement are supreme. It is not simply that God is going to punish the wicked and vindicate the oppressed, but that he has a long-term purpose of salvation and healing for the whole creation.

It was not until the later prophets of Israel that the full import of that phrase 'long term' became clear. The people of Israel generally expected that God would vindicate their cause there and then, but they came to realise that what Yahweh had in mind was something far more universal. That's why the story of the Bible ends with a new heaven and a new earth 'where righteousness dwells'. 'I am making everything new,' proclaims God. The nations, the unbelieving Gentiles, will be healed by the leaves from the tree of life, and evil will finally be removed from the whole creation. This is much, much more than a question of the destiny of specific individuals. It is, in the true sense of the word, 'salvation', which means being made whole.

I think I should at this point enter a caution (more for the author than the reader). There are two perils in writing about something like life after death. One is being so vague that no one knows what you're talking about. The other is being dogmatic about things which are literally beyond human comprehension. In the first case, there are many questions raised but few answered, or even attempted. In the second case the reader is left wondering how the author can be quite so certain about things beyond our ken. After all, it was the apostle Paul who wrote these words: 'For now we see in a mirror, dimly, but then we will see face to face. Now I know only in part; then I will know fully, even as I have been fully known' (1 Corinthians 13:12). I do not want to claim clearer vision than the great apostle, and readily concede that faith is not the same thing as certainty, and interpretation is not the same thing as direct knowledge. One day we shall know. For the present we are called to trust, but on the basis of our understanding of revealed truth.

Having said that, let us return to the subject of judgement. The word has distinctly negative tones in English, partly perhaps through the persistence of the old English word 'doom', as in 'doomsday' (the day of judgement) in popular thinking. In both the biblical languages it has a more positive tone. Here is the psalmist, in full song: 'The judgments of the Lord are true and righteous altogether. More to be desired are they… than much fine gold: sweeter also than honey and the honeycomb' (Psalm 19:9–10, KJV).

We don't usually think of judgement as 'sweet', but for the psalmist and the people of his day the thought that God was their judge, and not whoever held sway in the land at that point, was reassuring. Judgement, in other words, was equated with justice, and to a very real extent with mercy.

After all, the distinguishing characteristics of their God and Judge were lovingkindness and mercy.

In the New Testament the usual words translated as 'judgement' or 'judging' carry a very strong message of completion—determining, deciding, separating. They certainly include legal judgement and the infliction of penalty, but they also convey the notion of what modern people call 'closure'. We are accustomed to news reports in which people bereaved perhaps through homicide or an unexplained disaster are said to find 'closure' when a guilty person is sentenced or a situation satisfactorily explained. We can certainly see the judgement of God, exercised through his Son, the Saviour of the world, as providing 'closure' in that sense. Finally, all the loose ends will be tidied up, the inexplicable mysteries of providence explained, the ways of God made clear.

So what does it mean to say, as we do in the Creed, that 'he will come again in glory to judge the living and the dead'? It certainly speaks, in the language we have just used, of closure. It cannot be that the unfairness of life, the cruelty and dishonesty of some and the greed and indulgence of others will simply be passed over. That would not be closure but collusion. The God of the Bible would not simply say 'It doesn't matter' and let it pass. Before we can move on, the past and present must be judged. To a large extent, that is our responsibility. The best sort of judgement is self-judgement. Both the teaching of Jesus and of the apostles tells us that we should be slow to judge others but quick to judge ourselves (see, for example, Matthew 7:1–2; Romans 14:10). There is a school of thought which invites us to imagine what it will be like eventually to be in the presence (in whatever sense of those words) of a God of infinite goodness, holiness and love. Would not that vision of utter purity be, in itself, an instrument of judgement? In those circumstances, would any of us plead innocence?

At the same time, biblical sources also make it clear that God, and Christ as his representative, will be the sole and ultimate judge of humankind. Biblical images of 'the One upon the throne'—the *bema*, the Judgement Seat—are a feature of the visions in Revelation. Beside him, as he executes that final judgement, sits 'the Lamb with the marks of slaughter upon him', the crucified and risen Saviour, the one who 'takes away the sin of the world'. In that one vision the whole truth is captured: absolute justice matched by absolute mercy. These are not two Persons with differing agendas, but one Person, with the Holy Spirit, in the unity of the Trinity.

We are all familiar with the childhood cry, 'It's not fair!'— probably one of the first phrases most children master! Humans have an inbuilt conviction that things ought to be fair, but as we grow older we learn that whatever life is, it isn't 'fair'. It helps me, at least, to think of the final judgement as the moment when universal, eternal *fairness* is established. To put it another way, I believe that no one after God's judgement will be shouting 'It's not fair!' I think this may lie behind the glorious celebration in the Psalms of God's judgement:

*Let the nations be glad and sing for joy,*
*for you judge the peoples with equity*
*and guide the nations upon earth.*

> *Let the peoples praise you, O God;*
> *let all the peoples praise you. (Psalm 67:4–5)*

This judgement with fairness is not, we must be clear, a matter of people 'getting away with it'. The process of God's final judgement will remove from his creation every stain of sin and wickedness. His way of achieving this, however, is not primarily through punishment, but redemption. As a frequently overlooked verse in the Fourth Gospel expresses it, 'God did not send the Son into the world to condemn the world, but in order that the world might be saved through him' (John 3:17). Judgement, then, will bring, it seems, banishment to some but blessing to many, as they see the goodness of God, his 'equity', and their eyes are opened to his wonderful purposes. We may note that in the quotation from Psalm 67 the 'nations', the Gentiles, will be glad and sing for joy, because his purposes of love include them and all the 'nations upon earth'.

The last chapters of the Bible, Revelation 21 and 22, are post-judgement—the single divine act of judgement which is the general message of the Bible, and the two judgements (of those in 'the Lamb's book of life' and those judged by 'the books which are opened') in these concluding visions. They are a picture of the heavenly city, the New Jerusalem, walled but with its gates permanently open, a city without anything 'unclean, abominable or false'. Heaven would not be heaven if it simply provided a new location for all that had previously marred and polluted God's perfect creation. The judgement, solemn, real, but motivated by mercy and love, has brought about the final transformation. We could say, 'heaven's morning' breaks.

*If you insist on having your own way, you will get it. Hell is the enjoyment of your own way for ever. If you really want God's way with you, you will get it in heaven.*

Dante Alighieri (1265–1321)

# Chapter Six

# The kingdom of heaven

> *Heaven means to be one with God.*
>
> Confucius (551BC–479BC)

As we have already noted, the word 'heaven', in the Bible and in common usage, is employed to cover a variety of ideas. In the early books of the Bible it meant 'sky' or 'firmament' (the sort of cover 'up there' which shaped our known world), but even then it also meant 'where God is'. The God of the family which descended from Abraham increasingly came to see him as their own one, distinct from, and needless to say very superior in every way to, the 'other gods'. He was, of course, the God of heaven, his 'abode', but they saw him also as the God of Israel, which was his particular sphere of rule and government. 'He is our God, and we are his people, the sheep of his pasture' (see Psalm 100:3). In that respect he was like, but in their thinking much better than, the gods of the Gentiles.

At moments—at the burning bush on Mount Sinai, but also in other times of profound religious revelation—he was truly Yahweh, the great I AM, the infinite and eternal

Creator God. As the tribes of Israel came to the borders of the promised land, for instance, and prepared to cross the River Jordan into it, their leader Joshua told them that 'the ark of the covenant of the Lord of all the earth' would go before them, carried by the priests (Joshua 3:11). Other nations had gods and kings, two separate powers, but Israel had a God who was their king, their judge and lawgiver.

Later, when Israel-Judah adopted a monarchy for themselves (somewhat, it seems, with God's reluctant approval), the king became not God, but God's 'anointed one'. That is the language of the Psalms: there is only one supreme God, Yahweh, and the anointed king is his surrogate, carrying out his will and fighting his earthly battles. That went quite well, with a few very human failures by David and Solomon, until the disastrous end of Solomon's reign. Now there were two kings, of Israel and Judah, and over the years many of them are recorded as having 'done what was sinful in the eyes of the Lord'. The good kings stand out, but the overall picture is one of abuse of power, compromise with pagan religious rites and practices, or making unwise alliances with powerful Gentile nations. Eventually Israel and Judah were conquered by neighbouring great powers, the Temple of God was several times desecrated and Jerusalem occupied, and its people were taken into slavery. The promised eternal kingdom of David and his heirs had turned into an apparently irreversible disaster.

These cataclysmic events ushered in the era of the great prophets of Israel and Judah—Jeremiah, Ezekiel and Isaiah. Their message, at first doom-laden, but generally offering hope of a new and better 'kingdom' following national spiritual renewal, began to look for a new 'spiritual' kingdom, once again under the rule of Yahweh. The great agent of this transformation would be a messiah (literally, again, an 'anointed one') but now acting with direct authority from God. The hope of the Coming One became the one ray of light during the darkest years of Jewish history, as the land was conquered and occupied for 300 years, first by the Greeks and then, in the first century BC, by the Romans. The people, humiliated by their lot, clung to the hope of a new kingdom of righteousness under the leadership of this new 'Son of David', the promised Messiah.

Handel's *Messiah* echoes with this message, in the words of the King James Bible:

> *The people that walked in darkness have seen a great light: they that dwell in the land of the shadow of death, upon them hath the light shined...*

> *For unto us a child is born, unto us a son is given: and the government shall be upon his shoulder: and his name shall be called Wonderful, Counseller, The mighty God, The everlasting Father, The Prince of Peace. Of the increase of his government and peace there shall be no end, upon the throne of David, and upon his kingdom, to order it, and to establish it with judgment and with justice from henceforth even for ever. The zeal of the Lord of hosts will perform this. (Isaiah 9:2–7)*

This message of hope in a time of darkness runs through these great prophets, whose messages cover a period of several hundred years from about the early seventh century BC. For them the old 'kingdom' failed to live up to God's requirements and now he is to bring in a new one, a kingdom of righteousness and justice. The key to this will be a messiah, an anointed representative of Yahweh, who will be a true inheritor of the throne of David. Sometimes they seem to see this kingdom in terms of an actual earthly entity, at other times, especially perhaps in what is known as Second Isaiah, as a more spiritual creation, embracing people of every nationality. From this emerged the 'kingdom of God' (or 'of heaven', in Matthew) with which Gospel readers are familiar.

## The teaching of Jesus

The Gospels leave us in no doubt that the heart of the message of Jesus, whom they recognised as the long-promised Messiah, was summed up in just four words: 'the kingdom of God'. Mark, in his typically brisk way, pictures the impact of the newly baptised Jesus at the start of his ministry in Galilee: 'Now after John was arrested, Jesus came to Galilee, proclaiming the good news of God, and saying, "The time is fulfilled, and the kingdom of God has come near; repent, and believe in the good news"' (Mark 1:14–15).

Those words really signal the beginning of the Christian era. Only the Messiah could announce such a stupendous truth. The longed-for 'kingdom of God' was 'near' or 'at hand'. Its forerunner, John the Baptist, like a new Elijah, had introduced Jesus to the people. Now the teacher-prophet from Nazareth had burst on to the scene with this tremendous message. We have become so used to the phrase 'the kingdom of God' that its electrifying impact may elude us, but the crowds who flocked to hear Jesus knew what it meant. The corrupt 'kingdoms of this world' were to be replaced by a new kingdom of justice and peace. Entry to it sounded deceptively simple: repent and believe the good news. In fact, it was enormously demanding. Repentance—the Greek word means 'changing your whole way of thinking'—is never easy, especially when it is a call to 'repent' not a specific failure or sin, but the whole way we see the world. Even the closest disciples of Jesus found it hard, as we can see as the story goes on, until finally the cross and resurrection of Jesus brought new light, and the gift of the Holy Spirit at Pentecost provided grace and strength.

For Jesus the 'kingdom of God' was always 'at hand', or 'near' or 'coming upon you'. It was even, he once declared, 'within you', or possibly 'among you' (Luke 17:21). He holds it out as the culmination of God's purpose, the end of the journey of salvation. In the teaching of Jesus it is always 'now—and not yet'. We can become disciples of the kingdom now, and even united to Christ by faith and baptism, but the fullness of the kingdom is always just ahead. That is why, I suppose, it is (as Matthew usually terms it) the 'kingdom of heaven'. We are told by Jesus to pray, 'Your will be done, your kingdom come on earth', but the model for that is the location where it is already and has always been done—'as it is in heaven'.

The concept of a 'kingdom', in the biblical sense, is not a familiar one to most of us. The constitutional monarchy of the UK, in which the monarch actually has very little power though a lot of ceremony, is the precise opposite of the one familiar to the ancient world, where there was less ceremony (state openings of Parliament, and so on) but a great deal of power—indeed, total authority to rule. That model of monarchy, in its secular setting (and indeed in the experience of the covenant people, Israel), gave absolute authority to a single human being. The king made the laws, applied them, and was the final and sole arbiter of any appeal against them. The people of Galilee and Judea in the first century were only too well aware of the malign possibilities of kingdoms.

That is why Jesus taught so passionately about the nature of the kingdom of God, of which the Sermon on the Mount is a kind of constitutional framework. This was indeed to be absolute rule, let there be no doubt about that. God is king of the whole creation. The foundational kingdom prayer is 'Your will be done'. The difference lies in the identity, nature and character of the monarch. This is a kingdom where justice is done, but with mercy; law is applied, but with forgiveness for failure; judgement is carried out, but with equity. The king is the One who 'so loved the world' that he gave his Son to redeem it. Written in gold letters across the constitution of this kingdom is the magnificent explanation: 'God is love.' This was not a kingdom to fear, but to long for. We await its eventual coming in joyful hope.

As well as the 'kingdom of God', Jesus also spoke of life beyond death, as we have seen, in other ways. He sometimes simply called it 'the resurrection' or 'eternal life'. Once, in a parable, he even spoke of it as 'Abraham's bosom'—a fascinating concept for the modern reader.

'Resurrection' seems to have been used by Jesus as a kind of shorthand for all that followed from it. Perhaps the most dramatic use of the term occurs in the story in the Fourth

THE KINGDOM OF HEAVEN

Gospel of the raising of Lazarus. He and the two sisters who shared his home at Bethany were close friends of Jesus. Indeed, Jesus 'loved them'. This was, by first-century Jewish standards, a slightly irregular household (men were expected to marry by the time they were 30, and unmarried women were extremely rare, unless they were widows). Jesus, however, seems to have made their home a regular *pied à terre* (a second home) for his visits to the Jerusalem area. Of the two sisters, Martha was the practical one, running the household, and Mary the one who 'sat at the feet of Jesus', absorbing his teaching.

Lazarus fell ill and died. Although Jesus was told of his condition, he did not hurry back to Jerusalem, and by the time he got there Lazarus had been dead four days. The first greeting for him by both the sisters was identical: 'If you'd been here, my brother would not have died.' When Martha said this to him, an interesting piece of dialogue followed, as the Gospel records it:

> *Jesus said to her, 'Your brother will rise again.' Martha said to him, 'I know that he will rise again in the resurrection on the last day.' Jesus said to her, 'I am the resurrection and the life. Those who believe in me, even though they die, will live, and everyone who lives and believes in me will never die. Do you believe this?' She said to him, 'Yes, Lord, I believe that you are the Messiah, the Son of God, the one coming into the world.' (John 11:23–27)*

The statement by Jesus that her brother will 'rise again' would have been part of the religious beliefs of both of them, but one can sense the disappointment in Martha's response. Yes, fair enough, he'll rise again at the last day, but it's now I miss him. It's now he's there in the tomb. Future resurrection, on those terms, sounds a distant and rather academic response to our need for reassurance.

But then Jesus makes a truly staggering claim: 'I am the resurrection and the life.' It is, of course, the sixth of the famous 'I am' sayings in John's Gospel, and by far the most elusive. He *is* 'the resurrection'. That seems to be a cryptic way of saying that all resurrection is through him, that resurrection life is his life now made available to all. At the start of this Gospel the claim was made that 'in him was life, and the life was the light of all people' (1:4). The very principle of human life was exemplified in Jesus. One could say that he 'radiated' life. 'I came,' he said, 'that they [his "sheep"] may have life, and have it abundantly' (John 10:10).

The claim that Jesus is 'the resurrection and the life' is then followed by some explanatory words. Those who believe in him, even though they die, will live. And those who live believing in him will 'never die'. It is a breathtaking claim—in modern jargon, a 'game changer'. Then he makes it personal to Martha: 'Do you believe this?'

I have always admired her answer. While asserting her belief in Jesus as Messiah, she carefully avoids the claim of believing 'this'—all the complicated stuff about death and resurrection. 'I believe *you*' is the heart of her response, as I suspect it is for most Christians down the ages. We cannot ever fully understand the divine mystery of life itself, or resurrection life, but we can and do trust the Saviour.

These words of Jesus are the opening sentences of the Church of England funeral service. It is, I promise you, a daunting feeling to precede the coffin into church declaiming them. After all, as you are saying that believers never die, and those who have died will live, you are followed by a box containing—what? A dead body. There is no escaping the facts of the situation. Within an hour or less that body will lie in a grave or be consumed by fire. In what sense are they words of hope to the mourners?

Everything hinges on two words, really: 'resurrection' and 'life'. In the rather strange story that follows in John's Gospel the apparently dead body of Lazarus is restored to life. Wrapped in the burial cloths, he staggers from the tomb at the command of Jesus. In a very literal sense, he has been raised from death. Yet, at some future day, Lazarus will die again, and this time, presumably, he will stay dead. What was the point of it all? Resuscitation is not the same as resurrection, because resurrection is to *new* life, eternal life, life that will 'never die'. That is the message of the words of Jesus, and they have echoed down the Christian centuries. I confess that I do not really understand the physical raising of Lazarus. An acted parable? A gesture of love to ease the pain of Mary and Martha, his friends? The apex of all the signs and wonders that Jesus did? The fact is, it makes no difference to the life-changing declaration of Jesus. He *is* the resurrection and he *is* the life. That is why he came to earth, and why his own resurrection is so much more than an isolated incident. The world will never be the same again. 'Because I live, you also will live,' he said.

That brings us, at last, to the single word 'heaven'. It does not occur very often in the New Testament, strangely enough, and is usually connected with location. 'Our Father *in heaven*,' we pray. The linguistic confusion caused by the fact that the same word simply means 'sky' or 'firmament' doesn't help. The testimony of the New Testament is, however, absolutely clear that heaven—where God dwells—is the final destination of the redeemed. In the next chapter we shall finally look at that evidence—from the Gospel accounts of the risen Christ to the teaching of his apostles and the closing visions of Revelation—to find the clues it gives about what lies ahead.

> *What they do in heaven we are ignorant of; what they do not, we are told expressly, that they neither marry nor are given in marriage.*
>
> Jonathan Swift, *Thoughts on Various Subjects* (1713)

> *Heaven's gates are not so highly arched As princes' palaces; they that enter there Must go upon their knees.*
>
> John Webster, *The Duchess of Malfi* (1613)

# Chapter Seven

# Heaven

I gave a lunchtime talk to a large gathering in Henley on the subject of heaven. They listened attentively and at the end I invited questions. After one or two seriously biblical ones, from people who had probably been taking notes, I had three questions which I feel got to the heart of ordinary people's problems about the traditional view of heaven. The first was fairly simple (and very common on such occasions): 'Can I have my cat in heaven?' Substitute 'dog' or 'pony' and you have got the comprehensive nature of this popular question. There is, of course, no sensible answer one can give. The next one, from an older man, simply asked, in a voice full of doubt, if there might possibly be a golf course there. Again, there's no sensible answer. The third question I'd never been asked before: 'Will there be shopping?'

It raised a nervous kind of giggle from the audience, but in fact it falls exactly into the same category as the previous two questions. Older women cherish their pet, a daily and loved companion. Men love their sport, whatever it is, and can't imagine a happy and fulfilled life without it. And for many younger women (but hardly any men) shopping—'retail therapy', as they call it—is a huge source of enjoyment and even fulfilment.

In fact, all three share a common source: they are ways we have found to enjoy filling our duty-free hours. They are, as we say, 'pastimes'. Break that word up, and you get a simple conclusion. They are pleasant ways of passing time. In heaven, however, as we have seen, there is no time to 'pass'. Our new life, our radical new way of existing, will know nothing of boredom, lack of love, absence of excitement, or shortage of anything. So what does that say about our earthly loves, whether they be pets, or sport, or an hour or two in Primark? They are not 'wrong', just irrelevant. Deprived of them now, we would miss them dreadfully. But where there is no lack, there will be no regrets. I suppose I'm wrong to say that there's no 'sensible' answer to these questions. There is. Hard as it is to believe, we most miss pets, or golf, or shopping—or anything else—when the rest of our life is unfulfilled. When our lives are complete within the love of God there will be no need of 'pastime'.

## So, what awaits us at journey's end?

We have noticed that Jesus frequently tells us in metaphor and parable what the kingdom of heaven is 'like'. Are we now in any sort of position to draw conclusions, not only from those sayings but from our understanding of concepts like 'the Father's house', or resurrection, or eternal life, and from the teaching of the apostles and the visions of Revelation, about what awaits the Christian at the end of the final journey? Here are two passages from the New Testament, one from probably the earliest letter of Paul (written barely 20 years after the crucifixion) and the other from the final chapters of Revelation. The first offers what seems to be a factual description, albeit presented in the language and imagery of the first century:

> *But we do not want you to be uninformed, brothers and sisters, about those who have died, so that you may not grieve as others do who have no hope. For since we believe that Jesus died and rose again, even so, through Jesus, God will bring with him those who have died. For this we declare to you by the word of the Lord, that we who are alive, who are left until the coming of the Lord, will by no means precede those who have died. For the Lord himself, with a cry of command, with the archangel's call and with the sound of God's trumpet, will descend from heaven, and the dead in Christ will rise first. Then we who are alive, who are left, will be caught up in the clouds together with them to meet the Lord in the air; and so we will be with the Lord for ever. Therefore encourage one another with these words. (1 Thessalonians 4:13–18)*

Paul says that what he is passing on as encouragement to his hearers is 'the word of the Lord', that is to say the teaching of Jesus. He had met and been told these things by the other apostles, who had all met the risen Christ during the 40 days after his resurrection, when we are told he spoke with them about 'the kingdom of God' (Acts 1:3). That gives Paul's words here enormous authority, of course—though we must allow for the language about sky and air, shouts and trumpets, which were part of the Jewish tradition of the Day of the Lord and also of the eschatology (belief about the end times) of Jesus himself (see, for example, Mark 13:26–27). It is not clear how literally even the first hearers took this description.

The heart of this message, however, is not in such details but in the very clear promise that the 'dead in Christ will rise'. Those who are still alive on earth at this moment of revelation will be 'caught up with them', both being brought into the life of the risen Christ at the same moment. This was how Paul sought to reassure the Christians at Thessalonica about their friends who had died—after all, at that time they were expecting the return of Jesus, the promised second coming, at any moment. What then had happened to those who had already died? Would they miss out on the promised glory? The apostle assures them that there would be no difference. Those who had died would be raised, and those who were still alive would be transformed—it is exactly the formula the apostle was later to set out in his letter to the church at Corinth, as we have seen.

For present-day Christians two principles emerge from this passage. The first, specifically, is that 'the dead in Christ will rise'. The second is that all of this will be a communal and inclusive experience. The key word (v. 17) is 'together'.

The second passage is from the magnificent final visions of Revelation—the emergence of the 'New Jerusalem' and the new creation of which it is a sign:

*Then I saw a new heaven and a new earth; for the first heaven and the first earth had passed away, and the sea was no more. And I saw the holy city, the new Jerusalem, coming down out of heaven from God, prepared as a bride adorned for her husband. And I heard a loud voice from the throne saying,*

*'See, the home of God is among mortals.*
*He will dwell with them;*
*they will be his peoples,*
*and God himself will be with them;*
*he will wipe every tear from their eyes.*
*Death will be no more;*
*mourning and crying and pain will be no more,*
*for the first things have passed away.'*

*And the one who was seated on the throne said, 'See, I am*
*making all things new.' Also he said, 'Write this, for these*
*words are trustworthy and true.' Then he said to me, 'It is*
*done! I am the Alpha and the Omega, the beginning and*
*the end. To the thirsty I will give water as a gift from the*
*spring of the water of life. Those who conquer will inherit*
*these things, and I will be their God and they will be my*
*children.' (Revelation 21:1–7)*

This passage provides a wonderful visionary and poetic
illumination of the bare words of the letter to the
Thessalonians. This is the great final consummation of
all things, the uniting of the Creator God with his earthly
creatures in a new and glorious environment. For 30 or so
years in his Son Jesus, God had dwelt among his people—
literally, pitched his tent there (John 1:14). Now, in the
completion of his purposes, he is ready to 'pitch it' again,
to be among his people eternally. He will 'dwell with them'
and they will dwell with him in a new world. 'See,' he
says, 'I am making all things new.' This does not contradict
Paul's words in his letter to Thessalonica. Rather it adds
a spiritual dimension to them, a vision of what it would
mean for them and their friends who had died to be caught

up into the heavenly Jerusalem. Notice, incidentally, for those who are worried by such apparent contradictions, that in Thessalonica they were to expect to go 'up', and in Revelation we are to expect heaven to come 'down'. What's the difference? After all, 'up' in Berkshire is 'down' in Auckland for half of every day!

From these passages, and the general emphasis of the New Testament, I think we can form two lists. One is of things that will *not* be in heaven, and the other of things that will. In the list of things that certainly will not be there, we can list the following:

## Things that will not be in heaven

- Spiritual powers of evil (such as Satan and the Beast; see Revelation 19:20)
- Those who do or condone evil of every kind (Revelation 21:27)
- Death and its associates—pain, sorrow, mourning, tears and crying (Revelation 21:4)
- Hunger and thirst—physical or spiritual (Revelation 22:2, 17)
- Ageing and the passage of time—this is *eternal* life

## Things that will be in heaven

- God—both as the 'One who sits upon the throne' and as the Lamb (Jesus)
- The Holy Spirit, who is seen as the 'partner' of the Church (Revelation 22:17)
- The holy angels, spirits who serve God
- People—the 'redeemed'

- Recognition and relationship—Jesus and his friends after the resurrection
- Love and affection—Jesus and Mary Magdalene in the garden (John 20:16–18)
- Security and freedom (Revelation 21:25)
- An all-inclusive welcome to those who sincerely seek it (Revelation 21:24; 22:2, 17)
- An intense experience of *being*
- Joyful worship and service (Revelation 22:3–4)

The visions of Revelation are often terrifying, as they portray a kind of cosmic conflict between good and evil. The visions were given, and the book was written, for a specific purpose, as well as having an eternal significance. They were to speak to a Church under intense persecution, in which vast numbers of Christians (possibly hundreds of thousands) were put to death. They might justifiably have felt abandoned. They were certainly desperate for hope. These visions moved towards a climax in which judgement was fulfilled, evil destroyed and the final purposes of God triumphantly restated. For those reading it today, Revelation is a book which tells the same story of the kingdom of heaven, always 'now—but not yet', but still a message of hope when things seem dark and overwhelming, whether personally or globally.

This is not the old Marxist jibe about Christianity being 'pie in the sky when you die'. The truth is, human beings cannot live without hope, and the only hope worth having is one that looks for fulfilment beyond the present day. 'If for this life only we have hoped in Christ, we are of all people most to be pitied' (1 Corinthians 15:19). Christian hope is not a matter of wishing things were different now, but believing that the purposes of our wise and loving God will be fulfilled.

# Heavenly joy for modern mortals

From the characteristics of heaven which we listed above, it is possible to identify some which may speak as directly and attractively to modern people as they evidently did to people of biblical times. As I noted at the start of this book, pearly gates, golden streets, harvests twelve times a year and endless harping might not offer to us the appeal they would have done to a people who were mostly poor and struggling to survive in an unjust and frequently cruel world, and were used to this kind of imaginative language. It seems to me that five of the features of heaven we have listed speak very powerfully to five fundamental needs of human beings, whether they are living in the first or the 21st century.

*Recognition and relationship* assures us that in heaven we are not simply anonymous 'spirits', but in an identifiable way *people*. A defining characteristic of human beings right through their history has been their need to relate to and recognise each other. We are gregarious creatures, made to relate. It's interesting that many of our most negative words refer to failures in this aspect of life—alone, lonely, isolated, confined, cut off, solitary. It's true that at times we like our privacy, but we want it to be voluntary and scheduled, not permanent and inhibiting. It is reassuring to know, from the evidence we have examined, that heaven will be a place where relationships and recognition are valued. 'I' and 'you' exist, but so does 'we'.

*Memory* is perhaps our most valued personal gift. The human brain is able to store a lifetime of memories, some happy, some sad, but all making up the story of who we are and what we have experienced in our lives. Losing our memory is, therefore, a major fear and a grievous loss for human beings. So it is reassuring that memory is part of the resurrection gift—otherwise, how did the risen Christ not only recognise his friends but know the story of their shared experiences during his time with them on earth? The Bible constantly exhorts us to 'remember': 'Do this in remembrance of me' (Luke 22:19). Occasionally it tells us, 'Do not remember the former things' (Isaiah 43:18), and perhaps the erasing of painful memories is also a gift of God. In Revelation the vast crowd around the heavenly throne celebrates the One who 'was, and is, and is to come', the worship embracing past, present and future—but all in an environment where time is no longer a factor. Past, present and future in heaven are all one thing, yet the worshippers could recall God's past mercies as well as his present glory.

*Love and affection* survived the experience of death and became part of the resurrection experience of Christ. The most dramatic expression of it is the story of his encounter with Mary Magdalene in the garden of the resurrection— dramatic and powerfully emotional. It's the kind of story where familiarity tends to dull its power to inspire and move us.

Mary evidently had a very intense devotion to Jesus. At some time in the past he had delivered her from an extreme kind of demonic possession (Luke 8:2), and her love for him sprang from deep wells of gratitude. We cannot be sure if she is the unnamed 'woman' in the Gospel story 'who was a sinner', and who washed and anointed the feet of Jesus at the table of a wealthy Pharisee. But the words Jesus spoke then undoubtedly describe her experience of forgiveness: 'Her sins, which were many, have been forgiven; hence she has shown great love' (Luke 7:47).

On the morning of the resurrection, in the account in the Fourth Gospel, Mary came very early to the tomb of Jesus. She saw that the stone sealing it had been removed, and ran off to tell Peter and John. The two disciples ran to the tomb, and found it as she had said—open, and the body of Jesus no longer there. The Gospel says that John 'saw and believed', though it is not made clear exactly what it was that he 'believed' (John 20:8–10). The two men then 'returned to their homes', though they also seem to have met the other disciples, who had taken refuge in the upper room behind locked doors. Mary Magdalene, however, remained by the empty tomb, weeping. Through her tears she had a vision of two angels sitting where the body of Jesus had lain. They asked her why she was weeping, and she replied, 'They have taken away my Lord, and I do not know where they have laid him' (20:13). The story then continues:

> When she had said this, she turned around and saw Jesus standing there, but she did not know that it was Jesus. Jesus said to her, 'Woman, why are you weeping? Whom are you looking for?' Supposing him to be the gardener, she said to him, 'Sir, if you have carried him away, tell me where you have laid him, and I will take him away.' Jesus said to her, 'Mary!' She turned and said to him in Hebrew, 'Rabbouni!' (which means Teacher). Jesus said to her, 'Do not hold on

*to me, because I have not yet ascended to the Father. But
go to my brothers and say to them, "I am ascending to my
Father and your Father, to my God and your God."' (John
20:14–17)*

What is so powerful about this story is the interplay of two
people, one a young woman who was fully alive, in the
normal sense of the words, and a person whom she had
seen being put to death by crucifixion less than three days
earlier. Not surprisingly (and in line with several other of
the resurrection stories) she did not instantly recognise
him. One could say, he was the last person she expected to
see in the garden, though undoubtedly the one she most
wanted to see. He asked her why she was weeping, and
Mary repeated the answer she had given to the angels,
that they had taken 'her Lord' away, and she didn't know
where they had laid him. The response of Jesus was simple,
dramatic and sensitive, the one word 'Mary'. Instantly, of
course, she knew who it was: the name, the way he said
it, the tone of voice, the gentle revelation of the most
staggering truth. She obviously made as though to embrace
him, but he asked her not to 'hold on' or 'cling' to him. She
would see him again, probably several times, with the other
disciples in the upper room, and have further opportunity
to learn what his resurrection was to mean not just for her
personally but for the whole outworking of the kingdom
of God. She would not need to 'cling' to him in a physical
sense, because he would promise to be with them always,
'to the end of the age' (Matthew 28:20).

At that moment, Mary of Magdala, the forgiven sinner,
became the first witness of the risen Christ and when she told

it to the others the first Christian 'apostle', the bearer of the good news. What huge significance there was, then, in that momentous encounter in the garden—and what compelling evidence that affection and love, human sensitivity and divine initiative, are part of the resurrection life.

*Security and freedom*: Hidden away in the final vision in Revelation of the New Jerusalem is the sort of phrase that can be easily missed: 'Its gates will never be shut by day— and there will be no night there' (21:25). The biblical world was centred on cities. People spent much of their time in the open fields or the vineyards, but at night or at times of necessity they could withdraw into the cities for security. The walls which surrounded them, the watchmen on the walls, and the massive gates barred and bolted at night were the outward marks of that security. The inhabitants could sleep peacefully knowing that the city was safe from enemies and criminals. In the morning the watchmen would sound reveille, the gates would be opened and the people would resume the working life of the day. Of course, many people did live permanently outside the cities, but those walls and gates were the symbols of security, making the cities of the ancient world places of refuge in times of trouble and invasion.

Yet here is the heavenly city, the kingdom of God, the place we can call heaven, and its gates are never shut. They are, of course, open by day—and there is no night. The heavenly city is secure but free. Both the security and the freedom depend on the very nature of heaven: there is no evil, there is nothing to fear. Consequently there is a freedom that we have never known on earth. I suspect that freedom and security are qualities that modern people would value as much as their distant ancestors did.

*Belonging*: Much of the emphasis of traditional piety was on 'saving my soul'. Strangely, that is not a biblical priority. While it is true that we are baptised individually and by name, meaning that our profession of faith in Jesus is authenticated as our personal response, we are saved collectively. One cannot read the New Testament and miss that emphasis on belonging. We are 'baptised into Christ', meaning into his body, the Church, the fellowship of all who believe in him. We are not lone disciples but members of a vast family (the 'whole family in heaven and earth' of which the apostle speaks—Ephesians 3:15 KJV). We *belong*—to God and Jesus, and to each other.

The beautiful Greek word for this is *koinonia*: fellowship, communion, company, partnership. For many people, this is what most powerfully drew them to faith, or most emphatically confirmed it to them after its profession. I cannot think of the Christian faith in abstract, theological or creedal terms. For me it is people—the ones with whom I break bread week by week, and the vision of the vast multitude worldwide with whom I share that meal. As I have got older, I have also become more and more aware of that unseen 'cloud of witnesses' (Hebrews 12:1) of which I and my fellow worshippers are but a minute part.

The visions of heaven in Revelation are all of this glorious company. Finally, we shall be able to appreciate what a wonderful thing it is to belong, to be part of God's purpose for his creatures. All through the Bible the story unfolds, though we are slow to see it. From the beginning, the

Creator saw what he had made and pronounced it 'good'. His human creatures used their God-given autonomy to choose an independent path—the first sin was not to eat the fruit but to assume they knew better than God what was good for them. Then began the long process of salvation, through which human beings would eventually discover how much God loved them and to what lengths he would go to prove it.

First, it was two people, Abram and Sarah. Then, their descendants, the people of Israel. Then, from their ranks the long-promised Saviour, Jesus, with a message for 'the lost sheep of the house of Israel' (Matthew 15:24). Then, in his final charge to his disciples, the commission to proclaim the good news to the whole world (Matthew 28:19) and the dawning realisation that Jesus was not only the Jewish Messiah but the Saviour of the whole human race—he died 'not for [our sins] only but also for the sins of the whole world' (1 John 2:2). The last invitation of the Bible, in its final chapter, is for 'anyone who wishes' to 'take the water of life as a gift' (Revelation 22:17).

So the story constantly widens, until God's salvation (healing, wholeness) is available to the whole human race. The Bible's metanarrative (as they say nowadays) is the alternative revelation of an all-inclusive love which welcomes all who will respond to it, and makes them part of this vast heavenly family. In a world where isolation, loneliness and abandonment are dark shadows on many lives, this is heaven's answer. Come and belong.

There is a deep need in human beings to 'belong'. We tend to identify ourselves by particular groupings: national

(British, French, Chinese), or religious (Christian, Muslim, Jewish, Sikh, Hindu, Buddhist), or more trivially by our preferences (Chelsea fan, naturist, sun-lover, grandparent). Within our labels, we feel we are identified, given a meaning beyond our simple individuality. Needless to say, the Creator has comprehensively met our need for belonging, and there can be no better evidence of it than the ultimate 'belonging' of the kingdom of heaven.

*An intensity of being*: I have several times talked of heaven as a place where we will exist in an entirely new environment. The heart of that existing depends on God, who as we have seen is Yahweh, 'the Existing One'. In heaven all existence flows from his, because he is the source of all life, from the moment when the breath (or spirit) of God brought life to the first human being. Life is his gift—that's what those ancient creation stories tell us. However, so is eternal life—an intensity of existence which reflects the life of the One who is the eternal 'I AM'.

About ten years ago an unusual book made its appearance, rapidly becoming a worldwide bestseller. It was by an American neuroscientist called David Eagleman, and its intriguing title is *Sum: Forty Tales from the Afterlives*. In it he offers 40 stories about possible ways that we might experience that 'afterlife', as he calls it. He doesn't himself hold to any specific set of beliefs about these possible scenarios. He calls himself a 'possibilian': anything is possible, because we simply do not know what lies ahead, if anything.

The book is a fascinating, if sometimes infuriating, read—infuriating because none of his 'possibilities' gets anywhere near the intellectually credible scenario offered by the New

Testament. However, it is an interesting read, even for those of us who hold to a particular set of beliefs about eternal life and resurrection.

I was intrigued by the first word of his title: 'sum'. That is the first person singular of the Latin verb 'to be'—'I am'. As the philosopher said, *'Cogito ergo sum'*, I think, therefore I am. It struck me as an interesting introduction to 'forty tales', because every one of them, in vastly different (and occasionally frivolous) ways, is based on the idea of continuing existence. 'I am' is of course the holy name of God, Yahweh. It is also a phrase found on the lips of Jesus time and time again—*ego eimi* in Greek. The seven great 'I am' sayings in John's Gospel, which have been referenced several times in this book, are among them. But there were more, and each has a special significance: spoken reassuringly to the terrified disciples in the boat in the storm (Mark 6:50—literally, 'I am') or, majestically, to the high priest when he was asked, under oath, whether he was the Messiah, 'the Son of the Blessed One' (Mark 14:61). To entitle a book about the afterlife, however tentative its findings, with the single word 'sum' is making some kind of declaration about the nature of human being.

David Eagleman is an amusing guide to possibilities, but his title is intriguing. 'I am' rises above possibilities—though even a Christian would be wise to concede that while the principle of eternal life is absolutely central to the 'good news of the kingdom of heaven', the details of that 'afterlife' are yet to be revealed. We can say *sum*, 'I am', or perhaps more happily *sumus*, 'we are'. But, as the first letter of John says, 'What we will be has not yet been revealed.' However, his next sentence asserts that when we see God, 'we will be like him', and that must surely speak of sharing in his eternal life (1 John 3:2).

## Who goes there?

I can remember, when I was about six, my teacher at our Church of England infant school telling us a story about heaven. If you wanted to have a nice house in heaven, she explained, you needed to start now. Every good deed you did, every kind word, every helpful action would provide a brick for your heavenly house. But every nasty action, unkind word or unhelpful action would take one away. So some people would have very nice houses, because they'd been good. And some might have only a tiny house, or even no house at all, because they'd been naughty. She must have told the story very effectively, because today, 80 years later, I can remember it as though it was yesterday.

I'm not sure, however, how much it influenced my behaviour. So far as I know, I wasn't a particularly naughty child nor a conspicuously good one. Just about average, I suppose—shall we say, a two-bedroom semi with a very small garden? What the story did achieve, though, was to express in terms a six-year-old could understand the generally held view about entry to heaven, one that I didn't challenge until I discovered in my late teens what the Bible, and especially the New Testament, had to say about it. Still the old ideas persist, of course. Good people, those who meet some (unspecified) moral standard, those who go to church and say their prayers, go to heaven. The rest must take their chance, though at least where they're going might be warm. In the modern world, of course, many people simply adhere to the 'out like a light' principle. When you die, that's it—neither harps in heaven nor flames in hell.

I say that I held that rather crude but popular view of selection for heaven or hell until my late teens. That was when I actually came face to face with the teaching and person of Jesus. It simply isn't possible to square that experience with such arbitrary criteria. Even a casual reading of the Gospels will demonstrate that Jesus worked on radically different principles. It wasn't the 'good' people (religious and devout, like the Pharisees) who were booked for the kingdom of heaven, but, before them, the harlots and swindling tax collectors (Matthew 21:31). It wasn't the obedient helpful son who got the fatted calf, but the younger one who had squandered his inheritance on riotous living (Luke 15:11–24). It wasn't the cronies of the Temple priests who got promised paradise today, but a convicted criminal (Luke 23:40–43). It wasn't the self-righteous moralists who were set free, but a woman they had caught in the very act of adultery (John 8:10–11). Actions speak louder than words, and it is not possible to see this Jesus, in his promised role of Judge of the living and the dead, suddenly turning into a cosmic condemner. 'The Son of Man came to seek out and to save the lost' (Luke 19:10), not to send them to the fires of hell.

That does not mean, of course, that Jesus was soft on sin. Rather, the sins he denounced were not, on the whole, the ones we would put highest on our lists. The only person who chose to turn his back on following Jesus when invited to do so was a man who could not live without his wealth (Mark 10:22). The fiercest words of Jesus were reserved for some of the most 'religious' people of his day, the ones he scornfully called 'the righteous'. Those who 'passed by on the other side' while the wounded man was lying near to death at the roadside (Luke 10:31–32), the rich man who ignored the starving beggar at his gate (Luke 16:19–20), the hypocrites who judge others but not themselves (Matthew 7:4–5), and kings, high priests and governors who were more concerned with holding on to power than judging justly: these are the targets of the condemnation of Jesus of Nazareth. When he is, in some marvellous way, not only the Saviour of the world but its Judge, won't the same principles of justice, understanding, mercy and grace apply?

There will be judgement, as we have seen. But everything we learn of our God all through the scriptures tells us that it will be judgement with compassion, insight and mercy. One of the most common attributes of God in the Hebrew scriptures is captured in the beautiful word *chesed*. The King James Bible translates it as 'lovingkindness'. More modern versions often say 'faithful' or 'steadfast' love. It was the quality that the psalmists loved to acclaim: 'Your steadfast love is better than life' (Psalm 63:3). Those who see the God of the Old Testament as vengeful and cruel (which was how some of the writers undoubtedly portrayed him at times) cannot close their eyes to this powerful testimony to God's unchanging and steadfast love. Supremely, of course, that love was demonstrated at Golgotha, where his Son died for our redemption. 'God so loved the world that he gave his only Son, so that everyone who believes in him may not perish but may have eternal life' (John 3:16).

# God only knows

The short answer to the question 'Who goes to heaven?' is 'God only knows.' It is high presumption for any mortal to usurp that right. God knows, and through his Son, the Saviour of the world, judgement will take place. Everything we have seen of God as he revealed himself in Jesus tells us, however, that it will be gracious. Because he knows the human heart, he sees beyond our failures, obsessions, weaknesses, culture, history and circumstances in order to make a perfect judgement. It may well be that in the end he will ask us to judge ourselves (Matthew 7:2).

The invitation of Jesus in the Gospels is crystal clear: 'Come to me, all you that are weary and are carrying heavy burdens' (Matthew 11:28). He pointed out to some of his religious critics that they 'searched the scriptures' because they thought that in them they would find eternal life. 'It is they that testify on my behalf. Yet you refuse to come to me to have life' (John 5:39–40). As I mentioned earlier, the very last invitation of the Bible echoes the same offer: 'Let everyone who is thirsty come. Let anyone who wishes take the water of life as a gift' (Revelation 22:17).

There could not be a more generous or inclusive invitation. Just to want it, to feel the need, is qualification enough. The water of life flows from the throne of God and of the Lamb, our crucified Saviour. All we have to do is stoop, and drink, and live.

> There's a wideness in God's mercy
> like the wideness of the sea;
> There's a kindness in his justice,

*which is more than liberty.*
*There is no place where earth's sorrows*
*are more felt than up in heaven;*
*There is no place where earth's failings*
*have such kindly judgement given.*

*For the love of God is broader*
*than the measure of man's mind;*
*And the heart of the Eternal*
*is most wonderfully kind.*

FREDERICK WILLIAM FABER (1814–63), 'THERE'S A WIDENESS IN GOD'S MERCY'

# Chapter Eight

# Perhaps like this?

I referred earlier to a book by neuroscientist David Eagleman called *Sum: Forty Tales from the Afterlives* (Canongate, 2009). This final chapter of my book (planned long before I had even heard of his book) is a similar exercise, not relating to 'forty stories', most of them completely implausible, but to the one great story that has been my theme. It is an attempt to imagine what the experience of death, and then entry into the eternal life beyond, might be like. It is, of course, guesswork, and readers are free to dismiss it as such, or even to skip this chapter completely. It is, however, guesswork based on the kind of biblical principles about resurrection and eternal life which have been the subjects of the previous chapters. My imagined experience has no 'authority', and offers nothing more than one possible way in which we might eventually experience the glorious dawning of heaven. With that cautionary note, I invite you to share this imaginary picture.

## Journey into life

I went to bed at the usual time, not feeling all that well. I said my customary brief night prayer: 'Into your hands, O Lord, I commend my spirit.' Within a few minutes I was asleep. Sometime in the early hours I was aware of a sharp pain in my chest. Then it stopped and I felt a great change, as though something very significant had happened to me. It had. I had died.

'Strangely,' I thought, 'I can see', though I supposed not with physical eyes. I didn't appear to be in my bed, either. Around me a light was forming, a beautiful, reassuring translucent light, with hints of colour but absolutely no shadows. I was not at all frightened—more, fascinated. It was as though whatever was happening to me was under someone else's control, yet the feeling was of security. Then I became aware that the scene was changing. The translucent light was being replaced by a sequence of pictures. They rolled on and on and I began to realise that they were in fact images from my own life. Childhood, adolescence, early adulthood, work, marriage, children—right through to the present day. The sequence was not, however, simply of what one might call the 'nice' bits. There were desperately sad moments, of loss and disappointment, and there were images I would rather not have seen, of incidents I try to forget: when I was thoughtless, dishonest, self-indulgent, disloyal, unkind, selfish, jealous and bitter. It was, as one might say, definitely warts and all.

Why was I seeing it, this visual portrait of a flawed and fallen human being? There were the moments of great blessing: love, faith, worship, fellowship. But mixed in were these darker scenes. I would have liked to shut my eyes and blot them out, but I found I couldn't. And then I realised. We die, and then there is judgement. Well, this was my judgement, the judgement of the Great White Throne of Revelation, but I was being asked to do it. To see myself, not through the eyes of a carefully protected reputation, but as God sees me, was truly a moment of profound enlightenment. This was me, not as I appeared to those who loved me on earth, or to my fellow church members (or my own congregations), but to God. The pictures came to an end, and for a while my visual field was blank.

Then, however, another image began to form, again against the backdrop of glorious light. As I watched, humbled now, but still intensely aware, the familiar image of the cross with my Saviour Christ hanging on it filled the view. A voice spoke.

'If we say that we have no sin, we deceive ourselves, and the truth is not in us. If we confess our sins, he who is faithful and just will forgive us our sins and cleanse us from all unrighteousness.'

'If we walk in the light as he himself is in the light, we have fellowship with one another, and the blood of Jesus his Son cleanses us from all sin.'

So that was it, really. Judged and found guilty; judged and forgiven. As the great light again filled my vision, I realised that solely because of the grace of God and the love of Christ the doors of heaven were open to me. I waited— now, expectantly, for the next step.

Again, there was the beautiful, welcoming light, but now I was moving and realised that I'd got a body! I was joining what seemed to be an enormous crowd of people. Yes, they were clearly and obviously people, with all the marks of humanity, yet there was a difference, which I took a while to appreciate. They were not children, or teenagers, or young adults or old people. They could not be distinguished by age, though there were men and women. Of course, I thought, how could they have 'ages'? Time is no more, or its ravages. I wondered how this would affect recognition, but was instantly reassured. My mother, who died 45 years earlier, came up and hugged me. I had no difficulty in recognising her, even though she was not physically as I remembered her, but all the characteristics of her personality, and indeed of her physicality, were there. We were soon joined by other members of my family, including the one I most wished to see, my wife. There were old friends, too, and people who had been important in my own journey of faith. One of them, a very wise man, told me that these reunions would not mean that in heaven we would form exclusive social groups or relationships. 'You will find,' he said gently, 'that in heaven we don't "possess" people, which would be unfair to those who never had such relationships on earth. We are simply one vast family—you'll see what I mean.'

There was music and singing somewhere in the distance, but the immediate and irresistible impression was of a vast unity in love. The centre and heart of that love was God himself, not 'present' in the sense of standing or sitting somewhere, but embracing and filling everything. 'God is love,' I thought, and so heaven is love, too. That explained the all-pervading atmosphere of unity, equality, freedom, joy and love that pervaded heaven and was now filling my own heart. To love, and be loved, in a way I had never experienced before, was the prevailing air of heaven.

So I am in the kingdom of heaven. Not because I deserve it or have earned it, but because God is gracious. I am already learning that this is not an individual goal that I have 'achieved', but an overwhelming experience of unity in God with the whole of redeemed humanity. This, I suppose, is the 'together' that Paul talked about, the 'whole' of which I am an infinitesimal yet valued part. This is the joy of being rather than becoming, a kind of ecstasy of pure existence in the presence of the living God. This is heaven.

# Bibliography

Richard Burridge, *Four Gospels, One Jesus?*, SPCK, 1994

David Eagleman, *Sum: Forty Tales from the Afterlives*, Canongate, 2009

Paula Gooder, *Heaven*, SPCK, 2011

Dewi Rees, *Pointers to Eternity*, Y Lolfa, 2010

David Thomas, *Daniel, My Son*, Splendid Publications, 2015

Keith Ward, *More than Matter? What Human Beings Really Are*, Lion Hudson, 2010

David Winter, *At the End of the Day*, BRF, 2013

David Winter, *Facing the Darkness and Finding the Light*, BRF, 2011

N.T. Wright, *The Resurrection of the Son of God*, SPCK, 2003

## BRF

# Transforming
## lives and communities

### Christian growth and understanding of the Bible

Resourcing individuals, groups and leaders in churches for their own spiritual journey and for their ministry

### Church outreach in the local community

Offering three programmes that churches are embracing to great effect as they seek to engage with their local communities and transform lives

### Teaching Christianity in primary schools

Working with children and teachers to explore Christianity creatively and confidently

### Children's and family ministry

Working with churches and families to explore Christianity creatively and bring the Bible alive

Visit **brf.org.uk** for more information on BRF's work
Review this book on Twitter using **#BRFconnect**

brf.org.uk

The Bible Reading Fellowship (BRF) is a Registered Charity (No. 233280)